Is Heaven for Real?

Personal Stories of Visiting Heaven

By Patrick Doucette

***

Published by Kindle

Is Heaven for Real?

Personal Stories of Visiting Heaven

By Patrick Doucette

Table of Contents

Preface

In late 2012 an article appeared in Newsweek Magazine written by a Harvard-educated Neurosurgeon by the name of Dr. Eben Alexander. In this article Dr. Alexander relates how he had previously dismissed the possibility of an afterlife until he contracted meningitis and lapsed into a coma for seven days. While in a coma he experienced a life-after-death experience that forever changed his mind on what happens after a person dies.

He said that he had a first-hand experience of the "unconditional love of God" that was "as real or more real than any event in my life". He goes on to say: "I know full well how extraordinary, how frankly unbelievable, all this sounds. Had someone, even a doctor told me a story like this in the old days, I would have been quite certain that they were under the spell of some delusion."

That story inspired me to seek out the experiences of others who have also, through one way or another; gained a glimpse of the afterlife. I wanted to find first hand interviews of people who claimed to have visited heaven and document what they experienced word-for-word. This book is the result of that research.

Introduction

Ayrton Senna was a popular Formula One race car driver from Brazil. Tragically he passed away at the young age of 34 from a horrific crash that occurred during the 1994 San Marino Grand Prix.

Ironically the day before he crashed, another driver had been killed during the qualifying heat for the race; Roland Ratzenburger. Senna was a believer who often read the Bible; he was once quoted as saying: "Just because I believe in God, just because I have faith in God, it doesn't mean that I'm immune. It doesn't mean that I'm immortal." Apparently the night before the race, Senna was distressed at the death of Ratzenberger and upon waking, he once again sought guidance from the scriptures. According to his sister Viviane, "on that final morning, he woke and opened his Bible and read a text that he would receive the greatest gift of all which was God, himself." [1]

When Ayrton Senna crashed that day, one of the first persons on the scene was Professor Sid Watkins, a world-renowned Neurosurgeon, Formula One Safety Delegate and Medical Delegate, and the head of the Formula One on-track medical team. He later recounted: "He looked serene... I raised his eyelids and it was clear from his pupils that he had a massive brain injury. We lifted him from the cockpit and laid him on the ground.

---

[1] Pandey, Manish. "Ayrton Senna: The Faith Of The Man Who Could Drive On Water". The Huffington Post.

As we did, he sighed and, although I am not religious, I felt his spirit depart at that moment."[2]

I wonder what was the Bible scripture that he read on the morning of the race? Perhaps it was Psalm 73 verse 24: "Thou shalt guide me with thy counsel, and afterward receive me to glory." Of course that is just a speculation but from the account of his sister, he seemed to be ready, perhaps he might even have had a premonition of sorts that day. He left a legacy of charity and good works[3] and no doubt he is sorely missed by his family and friends.

It was reported that when Ayrton Senna was transported to the hospital, he was hooked up to life-support machines that temporarily kept his physical

---

[2] Watkins, Sid (1996). *Life at the Limit: Triumph and Tragedy in Formula One.* Pan Books. p. 10.

[3] The Ayrton Senna Institute, created in his honor has contributed over $80 million dollars to help under-privileged children since his passing.

body 'alive'. The story of Ayrton Senna passing impacted me in my heart; I felt saddened; I couldn't help wonder if he might have miraculously survived; I thought maybe his spirit met with God and he gladly entered into paradise at the time that was best for him. I thought of the scripture from Isaiah 57 verse 1:

The righteous perisheth, and no man layeth it to heart: and merciful men are taken away, none considering that the righteous is taken away from the evil to come.

Some people claim that death is proof that God is cruel or that life is nothing more than chaotic randomness, yet that passage from Isaiah reminds me that in the light of eternity we are all passing away in short order and we will follow those who have died very soon; even just a few moments later when measured with an eternal time scale.

Once again, reading the story of Ayrton Senna and how his spirit left his body inspired me to dig into this subject to find the most compelling, the most powerful and yet the most sincere stories from people who have had a glimpse of eternity and yet have returned to tell others what it's like.

The following accounts are from different people at different times and in different places. They are all sincere; they had a story to tell and they attempted to share their experience to the best of their ability. Some of these stories will likely resonate and encourage and inspire you. Some may be difficult to relate to or to understand; if that is the case, I would suggest you skip that particular story for the time being and move on to the next one. From researching this topic, it appears that those who have had these types of experiences; they are usually unique in many ways; even though there may be some general similarities.

Perhaps the afterlife is revealed to us in such a way that allows each of us to understand and comprehend the process of passing in a gentle way. The uniqueness of each experience may be due in part to the individual; their ability to take in the awesomeness of such an event may be reflected in their memory of the event itself. In any case, the following testimonials are presented to the reader in the hopes that they will encourage and inspire; my hope is that you will find, as I did, a common theme within these experiences which seem to reflect the powerful love of God towards humanity, towards us.

~ *Patrick Doucette*

Chapter 1 – A Miracle in Mauritius

The most amazing testimony of a young man, Ian McCormack, who was stung by the deadly Box Jellyfish; he was pronounced dead by the hospital doctors; they tied a tag on his toe and placed him in the morgue. He then found himself first in hell, and then later he was standing before God. Ian did not believe in either heaven or hell before this experience but he now testifies about these places because God gave him his life back.

I travel around the world sharing my experience with God.

I was surfing and I had a diving accident where afterwards I was pronounced clinically dead for approximately fifteen minutes. And during that time, my spirit got caught up in the presence of God and continually wave after wave of his love and acceptance began to flow through me just like a tangible presence of God and His light, just flooded me with incredible peace.

And as I stood in His presence and encountered more of God it radically transformed my life. Prior to this I was a non-Christian, I was an atheist and my concept of God was he was not real, it was all just fairy tales, it was mythology. It was obviously for weak people who believed in religion and couldn't handle reality. For me it was a transforming point in my life. I was twenty-four years of age, and I had been travelling for two years from 1980 to 1982; surfing, hitch-hiking around the world, through Southeast Asia, through Africa.

I ended up on a small island called Mauritius, sounded like a great surf, good diving; I thought I could retire there. I had sailed there in '81 and seen and gone back to it from Africa.

The fisherman I lived with were Creoles, they were laid back, lived off the ocean, and I just surfed with them and dived with them. And while I was diving they taught me to night-dive. Now I had taught people how to dive, I had instructed them, I was a qualified lifeguard but I had never night-dived and these fishermen taught me to night-dive. It was quite freaky you know going out at night.

We used to dive on the outer reef, in Mauritius it drops off around twelve or thirteen thousand feet, it's basically a submerged mountain so we'd dive on the outer reef from eleven at night to about one in the morning. And as we'd dive, we'd look with diving torches (flashlights) because the crabs and crayfish would come out and they are scavengers so they scavenge the reef and with your torch-light you could blind them and with your leather gloves, just pick them up.

So we would catch as much seafood as we could, sell it at the tourist hotel which is how the fisherman earned their living. And for me, I wasn't into the money, I was just into seafood so I'd go home, cook a bunch up, have a good feed you know, and then crawl into bed about two in the morning.

And there was such a variety of seafood, you'd get parrot fish asleep, you could choose seafood for dinner and well, there was just plenty of seafood. And we were basically living on these; when you travel for two years, you gotta live pretty cheaply so we were living on about a dollar or two dollars U.S. a day in small huts near the village. This particular night, we went out diving; it was a bit different, there was a storm at sea and I thought maybe the surf will come up on the reef, so since I dived for years, I talked to my friend and I said the surf might come up, it might be dangerous. He said, oh no the storm will miss just here, we'll go to a new place tonight, you'll see the best diving in Mauritius.

Now I was happy that I could go fishing, to throw out the bait and then reel me in and so at eleven at night we got our diving gear in the fishing boat, rode out through the lagoon across the outer reef, rode and poled our way down from Tamarind bay where I was living to a place called Riviere Noir, Black river.

As we slipped out it was quite dark as the clouds were coming in so there was no real moonlight and there was a little bit of a chop on the water. As I slipped into the water, my two friends had already gone in ahead of me, and as I slipped in something smacked into my arm and stung me; I wondered what on Earth it was, it felt like an electrical shock. Now the other two divers had swum off to my left and headed up to the reef; I had just been hit by something, I couldn't see what it was, it was an excruciating pain like electricity going into my arm.

I first thought electric eel; I thought well I've never seen an electric eel except in an aquarium, what was that to see. So I looked around the water and started making out these jelly fish and I thought well it can't be them you know, jelly fish don't do that, you know they'll sting you but nothing like that. But these jelly fish were a little bit different, they were bell shaped or torpedo shaped at the top, and box shaped with finger-like tentacles. I thought, well is that a jelly-fish, it must be, so I reached out and grabbed one with my glove and sure enough it was a jelly. Now as I grabbed with my glove, I had no idea that I had just grabbed the deadliest or second deadliest, some books say deadliest creature known to man; a box jellyfish; obviously because it's box shaped.

But I'd never read anything on it. I never heard about it and so here I had just had a box jellyfish go through my hand. Now this particular species in Australia is well known and has killed over seventy people. In New Zealand no one has ever really heard of them because it's colder water and further south. So these particular jellyfish are more in the tropical regions. And it's killed over seventy people, it's so deadly some scientists are now saying the venom is more deadly that that of the cobra, taipan or black mamba but as this jellyfish went through my hand I thought, oh I wonder what that is and just kept swimming. Then as I kept looking for crays, something else smacked into my arm. This time I saw the tentacles of this jellyfish going past me and I realized oh man, that it must have been what smacked me the first time by one.

I began to swim over towards the reef to talk to my friends about them and another one hit me and I thought gosh there's so many, there's heaps of them in the water. I had swum into a whole soup of them. Now jellyfish are hard to see at the best of times, because they're so transparent that at night they're very, very hard to see and they were smashing in to me.

As I asked my friend to surface, he came up, he says, "Hey man, what's happening?" I says something hit me. He says, "Get out of the reef". He had been swimming off to the left and the jellyfish are over here to the right and he hadn't seen them yet. As I put my head back into the water to climb up onto the reef, coming off the outer reef, just with the surge of the tide was a jellyfish being dragged back into my face. As I put my face directly in its path I had one shot, it was either going to hit me in the neck; all I did was roll and throw my arm in front of my face to protect my throat and got hit a fourth time. As the fourth one hit me I pulled the tentacles off and climbed up onto the coral reef.

This is low tide so there's about two foot covering the reef. As I stood there I looked at my arm with the torch and what amazed me was my arm already was swollen to double its normal size. Where the tentacles had hit, I had burn blisters and I could feel the toxin pumping through my blood system up into my lymph glands with excruciating pain. Man what's happening? My right lung started to be constricted as I stood there. Perspiration was pouring off me and it felt like a branding iron had been put on my arm.

As my friend Simon came out of the water, he looked at my arm and in French he said, "Qu'est-ce qui se passe?" What's happening? I showed him my arm and he said, "invisable!" like he knew what it was. And when he said in French 'invisable', I recognize it being the invisible one, well this jellyfish was sort of invisible, I though yeah okay. He said, "invisable, chok, c'est fini pour vous".

And in French he's telling me 'c'est fini'; means the end. One's enough to kill you. Now this man has been diving since a child and he was one of most respected fisherman in the village. Creoles hated diving at night; it took courage for a man to conquer the fear of darkness and night diving so I respected him for it. And so he stood there and I watched him turn the torch on his face and he turned white as a sheet. He said, 'How come you're not more ill Ian, this one kill you brother". I said, "I not know this one, you think I know everything? I not knew this one." He said, "How many hit you? How many cut?" I said four. He said, "Impossible, allez, allez, vite, hôpital."

Now this man loved me, I knew, he was a great friend of mine and I mean I knew, when he was telling me to get out of here, we had to move. And I heard him say hospital cut through mall, which is just out behind the village. Trouble is, I'm standing on the outer reef, miles away from the hospital in the middle of the night.

He drags me back into the water, the other night diver comes alongside me and I know that they have protective full wetsuits; to them the water is cold you see. To me the water is hot, my wetsuit unfortunately is a short sleeve vest with a long john, my forearm is exposed and my neck. The other divers had full hoods on, booties, I mean and full steamers, 3 mil steamers so they were fully protected.

As they came alongside me, they pulled me up to the side of the boat, the young guy who's a fourteen year old kid from the village, grabbed my left arm and began to pull me to safety. As they did my right arm that was just paralyzed and trailing in the water, got hit with a fifth one. As I felt that, I thought to myself, what on

Earth have you done, to deserve this kind of punishment or pain. I had a flood of memories of stuff I had done wrong in life. And here I am thinking well there's no use thinking about that whether I deserve it or not, I'm dying. I gotta keep my head together here.

They dragged the fishing boat over the coral reef into the lagoon; as they did, I heard them yelling to the young boy to get me to shore. I turned and said, "someone come with me, please help me". He said, "can't wait brother you die, allez, allez". Now I realized I was in trouble man. I turned to one and asked about my arm, "what can I do?" He spoke something in French I couldn't understand. "Je ne comprend pas", I do not understand you. He put his finger out and motioned with his finger to urinate. I though he meant to pee on my arm. I thought, vinegar, that'll do it; maybe urine would help like a bush medicine.

Peeling my wet suit off because it's constricting my breathing, I urinated on my arm and made sure I didn't rub the toxin in anymore and got changed into my sweats. My wetsuit was preventing me from breathing so as I got changed and sat down on the boat, I thought I must keep as calm as possible. I thought if my heart beats too quickly, the adrenalin rush will pump the toxin, hit my vital organs and I'm gone. I'm a lifeguard so I know what's going down. I know I need to get anti-toxins.

The way these guys are reacting, this is not some little joke, this is life and death stuff. As the young boy was pulling me through the lagoon, I'm sitting there as calm as possible but feel the poison move into my kidneys like someone stab their fist into my back. As the poison continued to move down the right hand side of my body, tinges of it are coming through into my eyes and I'm having difficulty seeing. It's getting blurry as I'm looking at the beach. I thought man this is deadly stuff.

As I hit the beach, the young boy motions for me to get out. I take one step forward and my right leg crumples underneath me as I collapse into the bottom of the boat. As I hit the bottom of the boat, I realize the poison has already paralyzed the right hand side of my body. The young boy puts himself down around his neck so I put my arm around, grab my right arm which is paralyzed and hang on to him. And this young kid does an amazing feat, he's only a small kid; yet he carried me up across the sandy beach which is really hard; up through the houses and the bungalows and the palm trees, up onto the main road.

As he got me there, he turned and yelled in French that he wanted to go get his friends, get his brothers. I realized he was afraid his brothers would be killed. So the kid panicked. I said, no ambulance, please, but the kid took off.

As I sat there on the road, the poison hit me and I started to feel real weak and tired and I had no idea this particular poison often kills within ten or fifteen minutes. This particular jellyfish usually takes adults down within ten or fifteen minutes. What generally happens is that they fall into a coma and simply never come out of it.

Here I am finding myself very tired, and very sleepy, I just lay down on the ground thinking that I'm just holding it together, as I do, I feel my eyes beginning to shut and as my eyes begin to close, I hear a voice speak to me. It said, "Son, if you close your eyes, you shall never awake again". I said, what? Who said that?

As I looked to my right I expected to see a man standing next to me, but there was no one there. I thought, that's bizarre, I just heard a man speak to me. I looked around, there's no one there. I used to think the mind is there, I'm not used to hearing voices unless you're in a straitjacket and a padded cell.

So I'm lying there hearing a voice speak to me but there's no one there. What did the voice say? Close your eyes, you'll never wake again; I thought that means death, you idiot, that would have been a coma, that's not sleep, it's comatose and certain death. I look at it now in hindsight, had I not heard that voice, I know I would have closed my eyes and that would have been it, I'd have died. I would have been like most of the others in Australia that have been killed by these things, slip into a coma, never come out; within ten minutes they're dead. And I was in peak condition, I hadn't eaten meat for years, I was a vegan, I was in top condition, not an ounce of fat on me but this poison was taking me down.

I heard that voice, I thought whatever it is, you're gonna die, so I stood up, fought off the death that was coming on me as best I could and found my left leg was still strong enough to support my weight. I used my right leg as a crutch and put my weight onto the left hand side of my body and hobbled down the road looking for help. All the lights were out, it's a deserted part of the island anyhow. All these big homes but the French don't come down except in the summer, you see. This is May and there's no one there yet.

As I move down, I could see a small petrol station, I hobbled in there and amazingly enough I see three guys, the petrol station was closed, there are three east Indian men in their taxis. I lean up against one of these cabs and they say, oh you're drunk. I said I'm not drunk,

I'm dying. I've been stung by a poisonous jellyfish, "sur la plage, invisable", I need to get to Cutmore Hospital. They said, uh we have French clients, the restaurant, we not need other passengers, sorry, sorry white man, cannot help you; and they walked away. I said, I'm dying please help me. They kept walking.

I said, "I give you money", they stopped. You know certain parts of the world, money speaks. They're taxi drivers, they stop. As they stop, they turned, one put his hand out and he said, "how much money you give me white man? I take you to hospital." He looked at his watch to see if he could pull another fare; while I'm dying here in front of him and he's arguing over the fare. I said, look I don't care for the money, fifty bucks, a hundred bucks who cares, I'm dying. He put his hand, "let me see your money now white man, I take you to hospital".

Well at that point, I'm thinking I don't believe this guy, I said look I don't have it with me. When those words came out, that was a mistake because all three of them walked away laughing. They said, "you have no money you stupid white man, what do think we are". They walk away. I heard this voice speak to me saying, "Son, are you willing to beg for your life?" as I heard that, I thought, beg, I've seen men in Africa beg; "yes massa"; I couldn't stand seeing it, from New Zealand, I've never seen stuff like that and so I couldn't stand seeing a man beg to another man but I watched these men walk I said, beg, I wonder if I begged, I betcha that would work; these Indians have never seen a white man beg; not in this part of the world. I've got nothing to lose, I'm nearly dead, I slipped down onto my knees in front of them; fell onto my knees 'cause my right leg was gone, my left leg was weak; lifted my right hand which was paralyzed and pleaded for my life.

As I did that, two of them kept walking lighting up a cigarette, they thought it was a great joke, the third one stopped and looked at me. I said it's dead serious, I'll die in front of you if you don't help me. I'll have the money, please help me. He walked over towards me, helped me to my feet without a word, put me in his taxi. I thought great.

As he took off towards the hospital, he turned to me and he said, "what hotel room you stay, I get my money from you?" What hotel room, money, the guy's still thinking of money. I said, I don't stay in a hotel, I stay in a bungalow, I stay on the beach with the fisherman. He said, "you lied to me, you're a tourist, you stay in a hotel". I said I'm not a tourist, I'm a traveler. I live not in a hotel, I live in Tamarind Bay with the fisherman in a bungalow. He said, "you stay in Tamarind Bay Hotel?" because there is a small hotel there in the village. I says no man, I stay with the fisherman, please I have the money. He says, "you lie to me, I take you to tourist hotel, they look after you, why you lie to me, why you do this to me?"

He didn't understand, no money, that's it, no hotel room, forget it. He thinks I've scammed him. He pulls off the main road, down into the village where I live. As he stops across from the village, there's a small

Chinese hotel. He stops and says, "you get out now." I said, okay, okay, I'm getting out; don't hassle me, I have the money; and I tried to get out. As I try to get out, my left leg I found to my horror was now also paralyzed; the toxin had taken my entire lower trunk out.

I turned I said, my legs are gone man, please help me up, I have the money. He said, "you get out now". I said, "I can't, my legs are gone". He took my safety belt off, opened the passenger door and just shoved me out. As I flew out the door I couldn't believe what was happening but I looked up to see when I hit the ground, my legs didn't make it. My feet were still caught in the door sill of the passenger side of his taxi. He couldn't close the door. I watched him lean over from the driver seat, shove my feet out, looked at me in the face in disgust, closed the door and drive off. I couldn't believe it, why on Earth would a man do that; for fifty bucks man. All he has to do is another five or ten minutes up the hill and I'm in the hospital. As he took off, I lay there and thought I don't want to live on this miserable planet, if that's how a fellow man treats a fellow man for fifty miserable bucks, I'm not afraid to die. If it's my time to die now, if my number's up, do yourself a favor son and die here. I'm sick of this place.

Now I lay there thinking that's it but as I lay there, one of the security guards in the hotel must have seen the taxi, he comes out shining his torch around the ground and here I am lying on the ground in a crumpled heap. As he ran over I heard the voice of one of the fisherman, I said that's Daniel. He spoke and I heard his voice, "Qu'est-ce arrivé, Ian ?" "What happened to you brother? Never see you like this, what you do on the ground man? What you take tonight?"

He thought I was drunk or stoned or something. And so he ran over and he's my drinking buddy from the village. I didn't realize he's a security guard, see, he was making a little bit of extra money on the side. You know, and so I pulled my sweatshirt up, showed him my scarred forearm; the moment he saw it he realized because he's a diver, "invisable!" I said, "oui,… oui

Daniel". He said, "Pas bon, c'est fini pour vous ..., you die with Simon tonight". I said no, he said "pas bon", he carried me in his arms, he raced me to the hotel.

Near the swimming pool, there was the bar and the Chinese owners that ran the place. They had closed the bar so all the tourists had gone to bed, but they're there gambling and playing Mah-Jong with themselves drinking whiskey. As these Chinese men looked at me, they said, "what's wrong with you? You drunk?" I said, "I'm not drunk, I'm dying, I need to go to the hospital, please help me, I've been stung by a poisonous jellyfish and as I'm speaking this, Daniel takes off into the night. As these men looked at me, I'm trying to explain, they say, "we no understand you, what you say?" I said, my arm, I pulled my sleeve up, it worked for my friend just a minute ago, thought if they see the scars on my arm, they might realize, I'm in serious trouble, so I pulled my sweatshirt up, they saw the scarred forearm, they stood up, "ahh, what you do, you stupid white man, you put the needle in the arm? The old man take the opium, why you put the needle in the arm, you stupid white man."

I'm sitting there going, where's Daniel gone; these guys think I'm a drug addict and I'm nearly dead. As I sit there, I see out of the corner of my right eye, my fingers start twitching; as I turn, I see muscle tissue between my knuckles going into spasms; within a few seconds my whole arm starts to tremble, it goes up into my face and my teeth begin to literally smash into each other as my jaw goes out of control. Next my entire face and body is in what I call the death rattles; muscular contortions, shaking to bits in front of them.

As this deadly shaking is going on, I watch the Chinese men run towards me and try and hold me down, as they do I'm throwing them off like rag dolls. My body comes out of these deathly shakes and I feel go through the core of my body an icy cold breeze; like very, very cold. I say, "I'm freezing, freezing". Then they ran and got blankets. They all thought I must have taken a poison in my stomach, he tried to pour milk down my throat. I don't know what he was thinking.

As I'm sitting there, I can feel the poison moving into my bone marrow, not the poison but death, icy cold death, necrosis moving into my bone marrow coming up towards my upper body. As I'm sitting there I know if this necrosis hits my upper body, I'm gonna die in front of them, I'm gone; I'm de-hydrated, I'm paralyzed, muscular contortions, now necrosis is creeping in. At University I've done various subjects and I got my degree in agriculture so I knew from my physiology I was in serious trouble.

I had to get to the hospital, I turned, looked in the car park of the hotel; one vehicle. I recognized instantly that is must belong to the Chinese owner who is now standing next to me. I said, "Sir your car, would you please take me to Quarte Bonne Hospital or I'll die in front of you, please help me sir. I'm nearly dead, eh, could you take me in your car." The Chinese man, looked at his car, he put his hand on my shoulder, he said, "oh my car, cannot run, how come so worry white man, huh, we send ambulance for you, don't worry, do not take my car, we have ambulance for you, how come you so worry?".

How come I so worry? Cuz I'm about to die mate! You ever feel like hittin' someone? I mean, I'm not an angry person or a vindictive kinda guy, you know what I mean, I'm not; I'm pretty mellow but I tell you what, I felt like punching his lights out. I sat there and every part of me said, "how can I re-arrange his face?" You know you hate it when someone touches you, you know they're in your space, he was not only in my space, he was in my face. I said, I'll hit him, I was just about to plant him one but my arm wouldn't respond; my mind was saying smash him, my hand wouldn't move. I thought great I'm paralyzed; I tried my left hand, it moved, I thought what on Earth could I do with my left hand before I died?

I thought my forehead, I could give him a head butt; you know I play a lot of rugby at home, every now and then you get in some pretty heavy stuff so I'm about to rip him down to my forehead; as I'm about to do that, this voice comes again, it says, "Son, if you do that the adrenalin rush will kill you, the toxin is too close to your heart." I thought, that's true. I looked away. I thought, if I survive this, I'll find you; I'm gonna get you Jack, you're history.

I'm staring out here controlling my anger again wondering what this voice was that had literally just stopped me from killing myself. As I looked away, tried to control it, my anger, I watched my friend Daniel come sprinting towards me; next to him another security guard. As they grab me in their arms, they carry me towards the entrance of the hotel and I see as they're carrying me the headlights of a small vehicle comes flying into the car park. As I see it come around, it's an ambulance; a small Renault with Ambulance written on the side of it.

The guy that's driving it doesn't see us 'cause his headlights miss us and it was a Creole that rang them so they thought the boys must be stoned or drunk or off their face; false alarm. The Frenchman driving it, changes gears and drives out without even stopping. He didn't even come in. As he took off around the corner, I'm slung between two friends watching this happen. Are you in a Grand Prix or something? I try and whistle but I'm de-hydrated, my friend let's me go and chases after the guy whistling a huge wolf whistle trying to get the guys attention.

Fortunately he stops him in the road, before he gets up onto the main road; the guy backs up to us, the other security guy throws me in, you know he gets me into the ambulance and we take off. As we race towards the hospital, it's on a ridge; they inadvertently put my feet in the front seat, my heads in the back seat. As we begin to climb the ridge to get to where the hospital is, the toxin that's now in my lower body starts to naturally drain down into my lungs, into my heart and I feel it starting sweeping into my brain. And I feel compartments of my mind literally shutting down with the poison, it's a weird sensation but I knew I was dying.

As this continued to happen, I start to see on the inside of the ambulance what appears to be a small boy with white hair. I see sections of some kids life with snow white hair. I then realize as I'm looking at it that this me. This is sections of my own personal life. I thought am I that close? With my mind I did a mental check, you know what I mean, of my own vital signs, my own mind told me, I am very close to death.

As I'm lying there thinking well I could be that close to death; I may not make it. If I don't make it and die before I get to the hospital, what will happen to me? Is there life after death or when a man dies is that it, finished; cessation of life? Well as a heathen, as an atheist I reckoned when you died, it was all over; the trouble was I wasn't sure; how many know you can be wrong, you know what I mean? Have you ever been wrong in your life?

Well I was a gambler and I'm gambling with my life here, I think hey, if I'm wrong here, I'm gambling; it's like Russian roulette. I could be wrong here. I have no idea what will happen to me if I die.

As I lay there, I began to see appear before me my mother. As I saw her, I was amazed because as I looked at her I could see she was praying. I think what's my mom doing here? As I saw her praying, she looked straight up into my eyes, she said, "Ian, no matter what you've done in your life son, no matter how far from God you may be, if you would call out to God from your heart, God will hear you and God will forgive you son." I thought, forgive me?.., God?,.. what's all this stuff about God? Is there a God?

I had no idea, until I returned back to New Zealand that at that precise moment on the other side of the world, my mother was on her knees praying for me. She was the only believer in our family and she had prayed every day of our lives, all the kids, whole family, every day, every one of them. And God had just spoken to her in prayer and said, "Your elder son Ian is nearly dead, pray for him now; and I thank God for a mom, a woman, who knew God and didn't give up on her son and kept praying even to the end.

I thought maybe there is a God and if there is, who is he? I seen thousands of them, everyone thinks their God is the right one; and when you're dying you'd like to know who it is, you know. You don't wanna back a loser. Not if you're a gambler. So I'm lying there thinking, I don't know. If there is a God, who could he possibly be? I laid there, I said, "God, I don't even know if you're real, I don't even know if you can hear me but if you can, I have no idea what to pray", you know what I mean, "could you please help me to pray, if you can hear me".

As I lay there, words began to appear in front of my eyes, it said 'forgive us our trespasses and sins'. As I saw those words, I though how on Earth could God forgive me? I mean, it's too late, you know what I mean, now I lay there and I thought no, God couldn't forgive me, I've done too many things wrong. I feel like a hypocrite even trying to ask that. My mother started saying in this vision, "Son pray from your heart". I thought from my heart? My heart is like stone, you could strike a match on it.

I said, "God, I don't know if you could forgive me, I don't even know if there's any soft left in my heart, but if you can, I sincerely ask you to forgive me of all my sins, please forgive me." As I said that, the words disappeared in front of me, more words appeared. "Forgive those who have trespassed and sinned against you." I said, that means to forgive other people, I thought, I can do that. I'm not a vindictive person by nature. "God I can forgive anyone, no matter what people have done to me, I forgive those that have sinned against me".

As I said that, the face of the Indian taxi driver appeared in front of me, I thought what on Earth is this man doing here? The Lord said, would you forgive this man for pushing you out of his taxi tonight and for leaving you at the side of the road? I thought, no, you must be joking, I'm not forgiving him, I was furious with that guy. And then the next guy, the Chinese guys face appeared in front of me. I thought, what on Earth is he doing here? The voice said, "will you forgive this man for taking his car tonight and leaving you to die in the hotel?"

No, as I saw both of these men's faces, I thought who on Earth is this voice? Who am I speaking to? Who's talking to me? These words, my mother called them the Lord's Prayer. Am I speaking to God or something? Is He actually talking to me? I don't wanna forgive these men; but man this stuff could be real.

Now I lay there almost in a catch-22 situation. Part of me wanted to just deal out to them, I mean I wanted to lay hands on those guys and not like a priest would do laying hands on them and saying, "God bless you my son", no I'm thinking like my hands going up around his throat and then asking him, "you're having a problem breathing, oh don't worry man" you know, strangle them. I mean, I'm lying here dying and I've got two men's faces before me and this is where the rubber meets the road; this couldn't be just some mumbo-jumbo- Santa Claus and the tooth fairy stuff. This could be real. I know that I don't want to forgive them, but God if you can forgive me of all the stuff I've done wrong in my life, and I don't know how you do it; then if you can somehow forgive me for the people I've hurt, I'll forgive these men; I'll never touch them, I'll never lay my hands upon them. I let them go and their faces instantly disappeared.

Fresh words appeared, 'Thy will be done, on Earth as it is in heaven'. I thought, that's God will, I've done my own will for twenty-four years, you know I'm independent, self-sufficient; I said God I don't know your will but it appears only a miracle will spare my life at this point. "God, if you are real and you can hear me, I give my will to you, I surrender my life to you, I will try and follow you all the days of my life if I come through this. As I prayed that, the entire Lord's Prayer appeared. As I prayed it, I understood each letter, as if I understood for the first time in my life that I was talking to God in this prayer and an amazing peace settled upon me and I knew as best I knew how should there be a God, you know what I mean, and He was real, I tried to make peace with Him, you know what I mean.

And as I prayed that prayer, the ambulance seemed to stop. You ever been in a car accident and everything goes in slow motion, well I felt like in that ambulance time seemed to have stopped as my heart was dealt with before God. And I had no idea how pivotal that prayer was, how powerful that prayer, prayer from my heart would mean in the things that were gonna take place next. I had no understanding really of how important that prayer was.

As the ambulance stopped, they lifted me into a wheelchair and raced me through the entrance for emergency. The first person who saw me was a nurse, she pulled my sweatshirt up, tried to take my blood pressure; as she pumped the machine up, I watched her look at the machine and shake it. I thought, what's wrong with it? She hit the top of it, turned to me and was like, there's either something wrong with you or the machine. She thought the machine must be broken, pulled it off my arm, pulled another blood pressure machine out, stuck it on my arm with the hoses, pumped it up and again hit the top of this one. She crouched down, started tapping on the side glass where the mercury is supposed to move for the pressure with her fingernail.

At this point, I can feel myself like in the third party almost like I'm watching this going on; now I knew this was not some astral projection, this was not some drug, this was death. I knew if I left my body it was a one way ticket and I knew that I was so close to death that I couldn't even hear my heart beating so I watched this nurse playing with the machine and I thought I'm in serious trouble. My veins might have collapsed.

The nurse just stared there blankly like I shouldn't be alive. The ambulance driver ripped it off my arm, pushed it to one side and raced me towards the doctors;

he knew I was in trouble. As the ambulance driver raced me towards the doctors, the first doctor didn't even look at me, he's got his head down going, "Quel âge a-t-il?... "Où habite-t-il?" In French he's asking me, "how old am I, where do I live", and I'm thinking well hurry up and look at me son, otherwise I'm not gonna be here; who cares about my address, I'm gone.

As he looked up, I thought he speaks French, perhaps he's not good at his English, I looked at the older doctor to his left, he wasn't looking at me either. He stood up 'cause there's such a silence in the room, as he looked into me, I locked onto his eyes and said, "Sir, I am nearly dead, I've been stung by cinq, five, invisable jellyfish, I need anti-toxins now, I'm nearly dead".

The nurse came sprinting in past me with the blood pressure results, passed them to the old doctor, he saw them and whatever he saw caused the entire acts of emergency come to life, if you've ever been in acts of emergency; you've got to be serious for someone to move in there.

As I watched these men run, I watched people appear from nowhere with drip feeds and syringes. Suddenly they started shoving needles into me; the doctor saying, "come on son, keep your eyes open, I'm gonna try and save your life". Anti-toxins for the poison, drip feeds, dextrose for the de-hydration, sugar solution. "Come on son"; smashing my hands, lifting my skin up and stuck a syringe between my second and third finger.

I had no idea what they were doing to begin with, then I saw my vein (on my hand) start to balloon out, bubble out and I realized they were looking for a vein which had collapsed. As they hit the vein, the nurse was so nervous her needle was bouncing from side to side. My vein came up to about here full of fluid, didn't seem to be moving. I watched this nurse manually try to massage it up my forearm to no avail; it seemed to be rolling off her thumb and forefinger.

I thought, man, my veins are collapsed, I'm in trouble here. I lying there thinking, this is not gonna take me out; I've been in enough sessions over the years, I'm gonna stay here and snap the back of this, it's not gonna take me down and I used every ounce of strength I could to keep my eyes open but with this perspiration coming down couldn't see properly, my lids wouldn't respond.

So I tried to lift my arms up to clear my eyes so I could see properly; both arms are totally paralyzed, they wouldn't move. I thought no; I tried to tilt my head to the right or the left thinking if I could move it enough, it'd get my eyes clear so I can continue to see; my neck wouldn't respond, the paralysis set into my neck; now I know I'm in serious trouble, I can now try and close my eyelids which is helping move some of the fluid but as I close stronger, I can feel the poison going back into the capillaries, into the back of the eye sockets. I can feel poison being pumped back there and my eyes getting heavier and heavier to the point where I realize if I don't close my eyes for a few moments and have a bit of a break here, I mean I'm gonna be no good for anything.

So I thought well I'll close my eyes, have a sleep for a few moments and then try again. As I did that, breathed out, a bizarre sensation happened. The impression of it was like there was a release or like the battle to stay alive had finished. I had no idea until talking to the doctors later; at that point they came back to find me with my eyes closed, took my pulse, I was gone; they had lost me. I was literally gone.

For a period of fifteen minutes, I was just a dead corpse, a piece of meat. And they had actually moved me out of the emergency room down to what looks like part of the hospital morgue or something; moved me actually bodily. In the tropics they don't leave a body lying around too long so they moved me out of the actual emergency room down into another part of the hospital.

And so for me I had no idea I had been pronounced clinically dead; to me I was asleep. The trouble was as I closed my eyes, you know things go dark, I suddenly found myself in a standing upright position wide awake. I knew I was awake. The trouble was it was pitch black.

My first thought was, "why on Earth did those doctors go and turn the lights out in here?" I mean, that's enough to spin anyone out, you know what I mean? Why on Earth would they do that? What kind of a hospital is this? As I stood there wondering how long I'd asleep for and why the lights were out; one minute it was a hospital room, the next minute it's pitch black. I though don't freak out, let your eyes get accustomed to the dark; maybe you've woken up too quick.

So I kept looking, thinking my pupils had dilated, still no light; couldn't see a thing, pitch black like a dark room. I thought well okay, there must be some light in here somewhere so I turned around three-sixty degrees, checking out to see if there was some light; couldn't see a thing. I thought, well I'll just go and find a wall. You know, find a wall here, get the light switch, see where we are.

As I went out to my right, I couldn't find the wall. I thought, that's weird, did they move me? Maybe that's why the lights are out, they moved me down to the general ward while I was asleep. I've woken up, the lights are out and they don't want to wake the other patients.

So I thought, well I'll go back to my bed, find my hospital bed, should be a lamp near there and that shouldn't wake too many people up. So I started moving back to the left, groping around looking for my bed; couldn't find it.

I thought, "great, ya idiot now you've lost your bed, how on Earth do you do that". You ever talk to yourself, I'm groping around trying to find my hospital bed; can't find it and another thought comes into my mind; it's so dark in here, you can't even see your hand in front of your face. I thought, well is it that dark? I brought my hand up. As I did, towards my face, my hand seemed to pass straight through my face, like there was nothing physically there. That's impossible. You can't miss your head, it's not that dark. See your hands.

I put both hands up to where my face should be; both hands seem to pass straight through. Then tried my arms, my body, my hands; as I went through different parts of where my form should be, there was nothing physically there; it was like you were outside of your body. But before I could think too much about that, I'm thinking well what is this place? What's this darkness?

As I stood there, I began to attune myself to it, I could sense the darkness had an evil presence; a cold encroaching evil pervading the atmosphere. Like it wasn't just physical but there was a spiritual darkness, do you know what I mean? As I, like there was evil in there, as I stood there, I began to sense something out to my right looking at me. In front of me, I felt like invisible eyes, something or someone checking me out. You ever felt that? Sometimes when you're walking home at night, you felt like someone is checking you out and you get a bit of a chill through your spine. Well, you intensify that about a hundred times over; I'm standing there sensing not only something but that there's something moving towards me.

As I feel the movement in this darkness towards me, I move back. As I do, a man screams at me to the right out of the midst of the darkness and says this, "SHUT UP". I says, shut up? I said nothing, what are you talking about; you know, responding to him; I brace myself for a hit. As I did that another voice of a man screamed at me from the left, he said, "YOU DESERVE TO BE HERE". I said, deserve to be where, where am I?

Another man in front of me, "YOU'RE IN HELL, NOW SHUT UP". I don't believe in hell, I was an atheist so I believed hell was just a trip put on people to scare them into their religion. I thought all religions are based on fear, if there was a hell, it'd be a party time; you know Ian Drury head-banging stuff. You know what I mean, sex and drugs and rock and roll kinda stuff. I was thinking that's what it'd be, party time. Everything you can't do up here, you can get away with down there. I thought I'd rather be down there than up there in the clouds with a white sheet on and having some, given some harp to play, you know what I mean and some little fat baby firing arrows at me. I thought I'd rather be down there partying than up in the clouds playing the harp or something.

But you see, both of those concepts just went out the window. I was standing, not in a party somewhere with the lads, I'm standing outside of my physical body; pretty hard to grab your beer down there isn't it when you can't find your face. I mean jokes aside, you wouldn't want your worst enemy to be down there. It's like I was standing there, it was like a holding tank; this is like, I mean this could be real, it's not the place where your physical body goes because I realized my physical body must be up in the hospital. It's like you're in the downline of reality. This could be the pit and these men are in the same place and your thought is like speech to them; you could be there from five minutes to five thousand years. You can't get tired, you can't tell time, you could actually be here, this could be it; as I stood there realizing I could actually be in hell in total darkness, I had a radiant beam of light pierce through the darkness above me.

As this light touched my face, I felt an awesome presence go through me and my entire body seemed to lift off the ground and be translated up into this light and radiance. As I'm being drawn up into it, I can see that it's coming from a circular shaped opening far above me; that this light is emanating out of a circular opening. I feel like a speck of dust being drawn towards this light.

As I'm being drawn up towards it I thought, "Is this real?" I looked back over my shoulder and far beneath me I could see the darkness. Somehow this light had pinpointed me and plucked me out of it. Still not understanding what this light was, I began to move up to the opening, enter it; as I was drawn into the opening I could now see that it was a tunnel, circular in shape.

As I looked along the length of it, I could see the source of the radiance. My first thought is, "this is the center of the universe, look at the light, look at the power coming from there". Then moving into the tunnel, I knew I wasn't walking; I was being translated through the air and at a supernatural speed drawn towards the light. As I'm being moved towards it, I watch as a wave of radiance comes up. As this wave of light comes off the source, it touches me and I feel warmth.

Comfort, all that kind of fear and darkness just seems to go out of me and I feel a living light move through me. As I move through it, from the darkness, I think where I couldn't see my hand in front of my face; maybe in this radiant light I can see something; so I turn my head, you know what I mean to look. As I looked to my right I saw my arm, my hand outstretched, because I mean I'm being drawn towards it, as I looked my arm was transparent; full of light, totally full of radiance.

I said, that's bizarre, I stopped in the tunnel, I said, I don't want to stop here, I want to see more. I don't know what's happening to me but I want to see what's down there. As I continued to look back towards the source of the radiance, I felt myself again move along the tunnel towards it. As I did, another wave of light came up and as this wave of radiance passed into me, joy, total joy filled me. I thought, that's awesome! What am I gonna see next, it's gonna be the most incredible thing a man could possibly see.

As I popped out of the tunnel, I watched now from a kind of constricted size and diameter of the light I could see; I now had unrestricted access to the radiance. As I looked out, I could see I was standing in what appeared to be the center of the universe; all light and power seemed to be directly in front of me. Shafts of radiance came out from the central core, a phenomenal radiance from the central core.

From there I watched this brilliant light piercing out and I thought even the stars of the universe, even the constellations must find their energy source from this focal point; what is that light? Is there someone in there, surrounded by this radiance or is that just an energy source in the cosmos, some power source of good in the universe or is there a person or a being in that radiance?

As I questioned that in my own mind, a voice spoke to me from the center of the light; the voice said, "Ian, do you wish to return?" As I heard this man's voice, I instantly recognized it as the same one that spoke to me on the side of the road where I nearly closed my eyes and died, the same voice that asked me to beg for my life, the same voice that spoke to me in the ambulance and asked me if I would forgive these men. As I heard his voice, I thought, he knows my name, there is someone, but return where? Where am I?

As I looked behind, I could see the same circular shaped opening like the tunnel I had just travelled down, dissipating back into darkness. I thought darkness, hospital bed, my physical body. Have I left my physical form, have I actually come up this tunnel of light; is this real? Am I standing here out of my physical form? Or am I comatose in the hospital having some bizarre dream or hallucination; am I alive or am I dead?

Well, in my mind cognitively, I could think of the two alternatives; you don't leave your mind behind. As I stood there grappling with what was reality, I thought this could be real, I could actually be dead. Maybe I did die, perhaps I'm standing here; I thought but return where? I responded to the question, I said, "I don't even know where I am. If I'm out of my physical body, I wish to return, I have no idea where I am,"... as I spoke that to Him, He spoke to me again, He said, "Ian, if you wish to return, you must see in a new light. I said if I wanna go back, I must see in a new light; what does that mean?

Light, see the light, look at this light, am I seeing the light? It must be, look at this phenomenal radiance; are you the true light? As I asked the question to the person who was speaking to me, words appeared in front of my eyes, "God is light and in Him there is no darkness at all 1 John 1:5."

I thought, I've read this somewhere, a Christmas card in South Africa, in Cape Town in Bantree Bay; I remember reading this but I didn't know what the '1 John 1:5' was. I thought they were hieroglyphics, you know Roman or Egyptian or something, I had no idea what that numerology was. But why these words had fascinated me was that it said, GOD is light. Every other philosophy or religion I had ever heard of or expound on said that God is Ying and Yang, light and dark, good and evil and the circle of life as they used say in their philosophy or in their religion.

God had both light and darkness in Him, they said you've got good and evil in you Ian, therefore if you're created in the image of God, then God must be like that. But this teaching said no, God is pure light; man might have good and evil in him but God has none, He is pure light.

As I stood there, I thought, could that be God? In Him there's no darkness at all, I've just come from darkness; whoever this person is, whoever this being is, there is no darkness, no shadow, nothing but light; could that be God? As I'm standing there, I'm thinking it could be, I mean look at the intensity and power that's surrounding Him, look at the phenomenal light and whoever He is, he knows my name and He knows what I'm thinking before I even speak He knows my inner thought; I thought only God could do that.

I thought if that is God and God is light, then His light and presence must be able to search my inner man; His Spirit must be able to see everything that I've done wrong in my life. You know you can put a masquerade or a mask up before people, you know what I mean, you can fool people but here I knew that all the masquerades and masks in my life were gone. I was undone, that there light was penetrating and searching the depth of me; I thought, they've made a mistake here; I shouldn't be here, I'm not a good man, I should crawl back under some rock or go back in the darkness where I belong.

I don't want God to see my life, to be transparent before Him and to be ashamed and stuff; I mean I've done stuff I thought no, oh, I've done that stuff, man. I just couldn't, I knew myself; I began to pull back and as I began to pull back towards the darkness of the tunnel I watched a wave of radiance come off Him and move towards me; I expected it to touch me and literally catapult me back into the pit but as this wave of light emanated forth off Him, it moved through me and all I got was love.

I thought you can't love me, I've cursed You; more love came, it came out stronger. I said, "why are you loving me God? You know what I've done." More love; I said, "I've slept around, taken heaps of drugs…" more of His love; I couldn't believe, my whole body tingled with a supernatural presence as love and forgiveness and acceptance just continued to issue forth from Him; it was like He was completely embracing me with His presence no matter what I had done wrong. I couldn't understand it, eh.

I felt myself beginning to weep; as I began to weep the love got stronger. I could feel this liquid love moving through me and filling me up on the inside. I felt the entire heart of my being filled with light but more tears kept coming.

I just couldn't understand that God could accept me as I was. I looked out to see that I was now surrounded, encased in radiance; my entire person was full of light and I was totally at peace. As I stood there, I watched the waves of light ebb and then cease and I thought I wonder if I could possibly step through this light that surrounds God; I'm so close, I wonder if He would let me in.

I stood there and said, "God, could I come in? I want to ask you the meaning and the truth to life." He said nothing so I had a peak at truth and love of how He could accept me as I am; surely He won't mind. So I stepped towards the radiance; as I did, I felt myself disappear into this light, it was so dense it was like a cloud. As I moved into it, now we're inside the light where is like shimmering veils of fluorescence. It was almost like stars caught inside this cloud giving off facets of radiance. Sparkling, shimmering like the facets off a cut diamond, how it gives off light but it wasn't physical in the sense of stones, it was actually light breaking forth in this cloud.

As I moved though veils of this light, an amazing healing presence was coming forth off the light; it was like a healing property was touching my broken heart, you know what I mean? I could feel my heart of hearts being healed. I mean I had looked for love and sex and stuff, but this was pure. This wasn't some degenerate, you know, sicko stuff, this was pure and it was just touching the depth of me; I know what sex and that stuff was but this was pure love no strings attached.

As I continued to move through, I thought is there any way God would let me see Him because all I'm seeing is this light; could I see God? Well I just see this radiance. As I moved in, it suddenly began to part; as the light began to open up I became aware that standing in the center I began to make out a man's bare feet; around his ankles were dazzling white robes, garments. Not garments of cloth but garments of light. As I looked out and saw that, I began to lift my face up to see the chest of a man and His arms outstretched with dazzling white robes as if to welcome me but as I looked towards his face, I almost had to turn away, as I saw the light and radiance coming off His face I turned because it was so pure.

And it was ten times brighter than all the light I had just seen. This light seemed to eclipse everything I walked in through, His face shone like the light was coming out in force from his skin, I could make out the form or the features like an outline but I couldn't see the actual facial features because the light was so brilliant. I began walking closer towards Him and I thought that must be God. I wanted to, like... just see His face so I could know who God is.

As I got within a few feet of His presence, I began to place my face into the light and it didn't hurt your eyes it was like you could look into it; as I placed my face closer in towards His face hoping I'd break through that veil; as my face did, He suddenly moved. I thought why has He done that, I got so close and I couldn't see His face. As he moved, all the radiance moved with Him and directly behind Him, the same circular shaped diameter like the tunnel was open in front of me almost like a cave entrance. I could see looking out from this entrance, incredible green fields, meadows, fields opening up before my very eyes. As I looked out, it looked like a new planet, I could see a crystal clear stream working its way through, it was like earth but untouched, you know what I mean, like a totally new Earth.

Every single part of me is going, "I made it! Somehow by the skin of my teeth, I have made it." I mean, I knew that somehow I belonged here; it was like I knew I was home, I was like, why on Earth wasn't I born here in the first place, why was I born on this miserable planet, because you must be born again in the Spirit of God, you must have a re-birth in your inner man to enter in to here; but I'm standing here and not realizing that's actually what had happened in that Ambulance, I actually had a re-birth in that prayer, that death-bed prayer. I had no idea that God had heard that and actually moved upon my spirit and washed my inner man as white as snow, crystal clear.

As I'm standing there, looking in, all I want to do is explore! I thought, my feet won't touch the ground. I could see the pasture had the same life force that was on the presence of God emanating right through it. I knew if I stepped on it, it would spring back, the light, everything was giving off life. As I started to move in, His presence came right back in front of me and blocked the way.

He asked me this question, He said, "Ian, now that you've seen, do you wish to go in or do you wish to return?" I thought return? What for? I wish to go in. He didn't move. I said, "I have nothing to return for, I'm a single man, not married I have no children- well none that I know of, please allow me in." He didn't move.

I thought of God, I mean my life, maybe I had fathered some child illegitimately; maybe I wrecked some girl's life and God knows that and He wants me to go back and father that child. When you're standing before God, you're not some smart Alec mouthing off; you know He can see you and you just want to be right; and I thought maybe I've done something wrong, I've got to go back. As I stood there, He didn't move.

I said, "God, I don't owe anyone money, please allow me in; no mortgage no debt, still nothing. See in my life, no one has ever loved me; no one in my life has ever truly loved me. Your love has touched my heart; I've never felt such pure love; can I stay here? I have no desire to go back.

If it was a way to manipulate, a trial, a hidden agenda or strings attached but your love is the most pure thing I've ever found in my life. No one has ever cared for me like that, no one has ever loved me like that. I have no one to return for. He didn't move. So then permit me to say one last thing, "good-bye cruel world and now I'm gonna take my chances and try and step through the light and hope that God wouldn't stop me. As I looked back to do that, directly behind me, God showed me a vision of one person who loved me, one person who not only cared for me but accepted me and prayed for me all the days of my life. As I looked, I saw my mother in a clear vision right behind me.

In a moment of sorrow, I thought, man if I am dead, what's gonna happen if I do step through. If I do step through could I tell my mom that I made it? Could I communicate with her from this place? I thought, no I don't want to risk it. If I am dead, and I step through, will my mother have any idea that in that ambulance I prayed. Will she have any idea that I gave my life to God and that God could forgive me; and I thought no, she'll think her hedonistic son went straight to hell. She had no reason to believe that I would pray. Why my life was completely anti-Christ stuff.

As I stood there, I thought God, I wish to return for my mom. I've lived such a selfish life; I want to return and tell her what she believes in is real. If I come back, you know I mean, if I go back, I'll find out where this place is and I'm coming back whether anyone believes me or not. I mean if anyone believes me I don't really care; if I died right now, I'm outta here, I'm going to go straight right up into His presence because I know I've made peace with my maker. I know that He has forgiven me, accepted me and I know that He will take me back into His presence.

Total assurance in my heart; no ounce of fear of death in me. As I stood there, I see God, I mean how do I return to tell my mom? He said, "Son, if you wish to return, you must see things in a new light." From His eternal perspective not my own, you see when the love goes into you, you start to see and love people from a totally different place.

I said, well how do I go back down that tunnel; as I looked back towards her, directly behind me now was not only my mom; I see now my dad, my brother, my sister; like a clear vision with thousands and thousands of other people I had never seen before in my life.

I said, "God, what are all these people?" He said, "Ian, if you don't return, many of these people will most likely not step foot inside a church any longer to hear my name." I said, church, well neither would I, I wouldn't, I don't even know these people. I know my mom, I wish to return for her, I love her. He said, "Ian, I love these people, I desire all of them to come and to know me." I was like, what? Here my heart is like, to look after my own and here God is telling me that His heart is for everyone. I could see just hundreds of thousands of people.

I had no idea what I'm fully seeing but I just seen the heart of God reaching out towards all these other people. I said, "God, well I don't know about them. But how do I go back down that tunnel, back into darkness and back into my physical body? I don't even know how I came here." He said, "son, tilt your head, now feel the liquid drain from your eye, now open your eye and see." I'm instantly back with my head tilted, which I hadn't been able to do, with my right eye open looking down the length of my body, to see my right leg elevated cupped in the hands of a young doctor who had been working on me. The fellow had needles and a knife in his hand, a scalpel or something prodding the base of my foot like a dead piece of meat.

As I'm lying and seeing this happen, I think, what's happening; does the guy think I'm dead or something? What on Earth does he think he's doing with my foot? I'm thinking, did I just see God; it was so sudden, would have been a lot easier if God would have let me float down from the heavens, down through the clouds, down through the hospital and back into my body. But I am instantly, as He spoke, I found out later that He has power that as He spoke, things come to life. I mean He says the dead can come back to life because when God speaks there's creative power in the spoken voice of God.

I found myself lying there looking at this doctor who suddenly gets spooked, you know what I mean, like he jumps, something's happened and he turns and sees my one eye looking at him. The moment he sees my one eye staring in his two eyes, he goes as white as a sheet and nearly goes through the ceiling….AAAARRGGH! I thought, what on Earth is going on? I watch him look again, this time it seems he's thinking maybe he hit a nerve cause there's a nerve in the base of the feet; maybe he's hit a nerve with the knife, hit a nerve ending caused the corpse to have an involuntary twitch or something. He's got an evil eye or a dead man's eye looking at him.

As he's staring with his two eyes frantically into mine, like maybe the corpse has moved. I'm thinking what on Earth is going on here? I hear the voice of God break through my thoughts, He said, "Ian, I have just given you your life back." I go what? No wonder this man has no idea what's going on; could you please help me tilt my head to the left and look out the other eye, I'm getting sick of looking at him. As I felt strength come back to my neck, it rolled, my left eye drained and ten feet away on the doorway were nurses and orderlies staring in at my left eye opening; they freaked. One nurse was crouched down, she jumped back and knocked the girl who was over her shoulder; nearly knocked her jaw off.

Ah, I thought, what on earth is this; I look back at the doctor, he's still holding a foot trembling, shaking like a leaf; although there must be a logical reason, maybe there's a doctor to my right ready to do a kickstart on the heart; I turn, no one is there. I thought, that's impossible, I look to me left, no one. Still the doctor is holding my foot and the nurses and orderlies are panicking. I'm going, you can't bring a man back to life by holding onto his right foot while gaping through a doorway. You need mouth-to-mouth or CPR or you know a kick-start on the heart.

As I'm looking at this, I'm figuring out, say, maybe I have seen God. When the doctors come and tell me fifteen minutes and start re-attaching the drip feed, I realize this is freaky. I'm thinking, if I've just seen God, that means my life has got to change. I thought, whoa, where do you start? I mean, where do you start eh, I mean I was a write off, where do you start to follow God?

I lay there realizing that if I've been dead that long, I could be on a machine; I thought maybe I'll never even get out of the hospital if I've been dead that long. I thought, God if you've just given me my life back, could you please do another miracle, could you please heal me and allow me to walk out of this hospital and live a normal life; if not I'd rather be dead, please take me back into your presence. I'd rather be dead than on a machine.

As I lay there, I felt this warmth and power almost in the natural like electricity but I now know it to be the supernatural presence of God. As this power-like electricity began to move through me in successive waves, I felt healing move into me and within three or four hours, I got total movement and feeling back.

They moved me to the general ward, and the next day I discharged myself from the hospital, walked out under my own steam completely healed. I believe in the supernatural healing power of God. As I walked out the fishermen in the village saw me come back into the village and thought I was a ghost come back from the dead to haunt them; they ran! Some picked up stones and called me a spirit; they thought I was a spirit coming back to torment them.

I began immediately to see in the supernatural realm. I began to look at people and know what was going on in their life; see what was oppressing them, what was coming against them and I thought why is that? He said you're seeing people in a new light, He said don't judge people, I want to heal them, set them free from the darkness and oppression that's harming them; I want to see them set free out of darkness and brought into My light. I said, God what am I, what's going on? I'm not chasing ladies anymore, I don't want to party, I don't want to get drunk or stoned, every part of me wants to live a pure life.

It's a radical change for me, what's happened to me? He said, Ian, you are a re-born Christian; that prayer in that ambulance saved your soul, son, I said God what must I do then? He said, read a Bible. I thought well I don't even know what re-born Christian is, I've never read a Bible. He said, you're father's got one back in New Zealand.

For the first time in my life, I asked my dad for a bible, he had one stashed away in the closet. He pulled it out gave it to me and within six weeks, I read the entire scriptures from Genesis to Revelation. As I read it, I began to weep, I thought Ian you arrogant pig, you've mocked this stuff out from a distance, you have foul-mouthed it, you have cursed God, you have never taken the time to read this book. You fool. As I read, I began to see stuff I had seen mentioned in the scriptures.

As I began to read, I said God, what happened to me? He said, Ian, in that ambulance, you prayed a prayer out of Matthew chapter six, that prayer was called the Lord's Prayer; that prayer, prayed from your heart, saved your soul. You asked forgiveness of your sins, I forgave you right there.

I said why did it have to be a Chinese and Indian man? He said, Ian because if you don't forgive others who have sinned against you, you will have bitterness and anger and hatred and revenge in your heart is like a cancer, it will eat you up. But if you forgive others who have sinned against you, I can then come and heal your broken heart. He said, Matthew 6, 14 and 15, you must forgive others that have sinned against you.

He said on the cross I forgave those who crucified myself, I said Father forgive them for they know not what they do. I said God, what was that thing about Lordship? He said, when you gave your will to me, you made me lord, when you asked forgiveness I became your savior. Those who call upon the name of the Lord, shall be saved Romans chapter ten. He said, that death bed prayer saved your soul right there in the ambulance.

I said God, then what's this thing, I seemed to leave my body or something. He said Ecclesiastes 12 verse 7 when a man dies, his spirit leaves his body and returns to God. His physical body, God says, is mere ash and dust. I said I seemed to go through darkness, where is that mentioned in the Bible. He said, Acts 26 verse 18, Jude chapter 1, Second Peter chapter 2, there is a kingdom of darkness which is ruled by Lucifer, Satan and He said but there is a kingdom of light ruled by my Son.

I said, then why did you take me through the darkness? He said, Ian, I took you through the darkness to show you where you should have gone, had you not prayed in the ambulance and given your life to me, I would have left you in the darkness until the day of judgment. You would have been held in chains of darkness until then. I said God, in that darkness men were screaming at me. He said that's right, other have been judged and are left there until the final day of judgment. I said then why did you take me out? He said, well you prayed son, I took you through the valley of the shadow of death and deep darkness, Psalm 23 but evil could not touch you because you made me your personal Lord and Shepherd just before you died.

I said God, the light, He said, John 1 verse 5, the light shines in the darkness and the darkness flees, does not comprehend. He said those walking in darkness, Luke 1, 79 have seen a great light and God has guided their feet into the paths of peace and righteousness. He said those walking in darkness have seen a great light. He said where could you go from my presence, Psalm 139. Even if he descends to the lower regions of the Earth, yet shall I pursue you.

He said, God often does this with man, He brings them back from the pit that they might be redeemed and that they might be enlightened with the light of life. Job 33, I think it's verse 23 on, 23 to 25.

I said God a tunnel, where is that mentioned? He said, Matthew 7, 13 and 14 narrow and small is the way that leads unto the presence of God, you found it; most find the broad way that leads to destruction and outer darkness. He said, son, I took you along the highway of holiness. I say God, I seen waves of love and joy, comfort and peace. He said Galatians chapter 5, the fruit of my Holy Spirit is love, peace and joy. He said, my Spirit gives off love, my Spirit gives off peace, life, eternal life, resurrection life for those who believe in me. I said I couldn't see my body; He said you are a spirit being created in my image, God is a Spirit and we are created in His form; He said you will not receive your heavenly body until my second coming; He said then the dead in Christ shall rise and you shall be with Me throughout eternity and your spirit being will be covered with a new resurrected, glorified, heavenly body.

I said I moved through the tunnel and a man was standing there in white light that filled the universe, who was that? He said, that was my Son, Jesus; I said where is that mentioned? He said, John chapter 8 verse 12, Jesus clearly taught He was the light of the world; those who came to Him should no longer walk in darkness but have the light of life. See, on the mount of transfiguration, Jesus' face began to shine with radiance like light and His garments were gleaming white light. He said, that was a picture of what I was gonna do for my Son when He rose from the dead and was to be glorified. He said, what you saw is my glorified Son.

I said oh right, Revelation 21 verse 23, the light that surrounds Jesus, the light of the world, is so bright that in the new heavens and the new Earth, you'll not need the light of the sun or the light of the moon or the light of a lamp because the radiance and glory that comes off Christ the Lamb of God shall fill eternity.

I said, God I stepped through that light; how could I do that? He said, Ian the veil has been torn into the holy of holies through the blood of Jesus, through His sacrifice; we have entry in to the holy place to look upon His form and glory, 2 Corinthians chapter 3 and be transformed in the inner man from glory to glory. He said you could look upon His form, His glory, but not look upon His face.

I said, why? He said, no man looks upon the face of God and lives. I said, what if I had seen His face? He said, you will see that only when you step through and stay in eternity; Revelation 22 verse 4, we shall see Him face to face in eternity. I said God, He moved to one side and He stepped aside; My Son clearly taught He was the door of life; the door of life, the door to the sheep; John 10 verse 7 to 9 and He said, those who came into Him shall be saved and go in and out and find green pasture.

I said, it was like a door, or like a window into eternity. He said, that's right at the end of the tunnel, there was the door of life where nothing unclean, nothing of darkness can enter in; unless I know you, you cannot enter in. He said it's not just words, it must be the heart; He said I know the heart of man; men honor me with their lips but their heart is far from me. He said, only if you give your heart to me which is the greatest commandment to love the Lord your God with all your heart, with all thy soul, with all thy strength; until you do that, you cannot be born again.

It's done from your heart, from your spirit, not just from your intellect; it's not just an intellectual extension; it's a heart desire to worship Me.

I said, I saw God, He stepped aside and let me through, he said 2 peter chapter 3, 10 to 18 , God said I have prepared a new heaven and a new Earth for those who love me. Jesus said, "I go and prepare a place for you; if it wasn't so, I would have told you" and I said, I saw a river, He said a river of life; I saw a totally new planet. He said, Ian that is set before those who love Me. He said, this old heaven and this old Earth will pass away in an all consuming fire, it will melt, the elements will melt, but your spirit will pass through the fire and come through into glory.

I said, God, I looked behind me, I saw people, thousands of them. He said 2 Peter chapter 3 verse 9, I wish that no one would perish, that all mankind would come to know me; every man woman and child would have an opportunity to know my unconditional love and acceptance, be born again of My Spirit, come to the foot of the cross, the throne of grace and find help in their time of need.

He said, you can boldly come to the throne of grace and find help in your time of need. I said, I seemed to go back into my body, what's that? He said, I am the resurrection and the life, those who believe in Me, though they die yet shall they live. He said, I have power to speak a human spirit back into their body; I rose Lazarus from the dead who had been dead four days and said "Lazarus, come forth" when I spoke his spirit instantly came back into his dead body and he walked out. When I spoke, the worlds came into existence; I am the Word of God.

I am the Living Word of God. My Son is the Living Word of God made flesh. I said, then who is Jesus? He said, Jesus is God, He said, when you've seen Jesus, you've seen the Father, God, the invisible Father in human form. He is the visible form of the invisible God. He said, every knee shall bow and every tongue confess that Jesus Christ is Lord. I said, what are you saying? He said, Ian there is only one name by which man might be saved Acts 4 verse 12, there is no other name given under heaven or on Earth amongst men by which you might be saved, except the name of Jesus.

I said, people say there are hundreds of ways through, Christianity is only one of the pathways, what do you say? He said, John 14 verse 6 clearly taught through the scriptures, Jesus said, "I am the way", I am the truth, I am the light, no one comes to Me but through my son Jesus. He said there is only one pathway, one passageway that brings people into my presence.

I said, hundreds of people see that light, move along that tunnel, but don't believe it's you; why is that? He said, Ian, even Lucifer, even Satan can come as an angel of light and deceive people into believing there is something else. He said, even if an angel or another spirit would come and preach anything but Christ, let him be accursed because there are many spirits but there is only one Spirit that is holy, the same Spirit that rose my Son Jesus from the dead.

He said, I want my Son's Spirit, the Holy Spirit to dwell with your spirit for you to be adopted, one with me, one with the Father. I said, people say that Jesus is one of the faces of God. He said, no son, when you have seen Jesus, you have the incarnate face of God in human form. When you seen Jesus, He is God, all the other teachers of other religions were mere men, they never proclaimed to be God. Jesus is the only teacher, the only prophet, the only person to declare, I am God; they crucified Him. He prophesied, if I die, I will rise from the dead.

All the other teachers you will find their bodies spread from here to Katmandu. But you'll not find the body or the bones of Jesus. Why, you go into Jerusalem, He has risen, He is no longer there; why? Because that same resurrection power that rose Christ from the dead will raise those who believe upon Him into eternal life; that the power of God will take your human spirit up into glory. I thought that's phenomenal! I said, I saw my mother. He said, that's right your mother was praying, her intercessory prayers broke into that ambulance. I said, could she have repented for me? He said, no, she could not have prayed you out of hell and she could not have prayed the prayer of salvation. You must pray yourself and be born again of My Spirit; John chapter 3 verse 3.

I said God, people want to know you but how do they do that? He said, Ian, by asking for forgiveness of their sins. He said, what separates mankind from Me a holy God isn't that I don't love them, I love their person; the sins that they do, the evil that they do, the pride, the arrogance, the lust, the perversion, the adultery, the drunkenness, the death, the murder that they commit. They have been driven and talked to and listened to powers of darkness. He said men that have murdered and slaughtered children and butchered them have been inspired and taken over by demonic powers; but I have come to set man free from the power of Satan, the power of evil spirits to bring them out of bondage; to bring them out of the occult; to bring them into the light of my radiance.

He said, if a man would choose to follow Me, I will set him free; he whom the Son of God sets free, is free indeed. He said, that's why every demon on this planet must acknowledge the name of Jesus. There are people that are demon possessed; we lock them up and put them in strait-jackets but they can be set free in the name of Jesus.

He said, I have conquered death, I have conquered Lucifer; on the cross I have taken back the keys of death and Hades. He said, what you saw on that person, the radiant robe; yes, I said, where is that? He said, Revelation chapter 1 verse 13 to 18 in the midst of the lampstands stood the Son of Man with white robes reaching His feet; I said, I saw that! His head of hair was white like wool, like snow and His face shone like the sun in full strength, in His right hand he held seven stars; His eyes are like a flame of fire and his voice is like the sound of many waters.

I said, who was that? He said, do not be afraid, I was dead but behold I am alive forevermore. I hold the keys of death and hades, death and hell, I am the resurrected, glorified Son of Almighty God. Yeshua, Ha-Mashiach, the Messiah. I am the King of Kings and Lord of Lords, I am the Alpha and the Omega, the beginning and the end; I am Jesus, Son of God, glorified the eternal master of the universe and I thought; I saw Jesus! That was written two thousand years ago, that's right, that vision was a vision of Revelation of one of my Apostles, John on the island of Patmos in the Greek island he was caught up unto the radiant presence of God and saw me in my glorified form.

He said, what you saw is the same picture that John saw; I said, well who am I? He said, son, you were a man walking in darkness and evil, your life was full of evil but you were whole-hearted, so I revealed myself to you. I said, people won't believe. That's right, when I rose from the dead people refused to believe Me, they still lie about Me today but I have risen from the dead.

I said, is there anyone in the Bible that had an experience like me? He said, 2 Corinthians chapter 12 verse 2 to 4 Paul said I knew a man in Christ who fourteen years ago whether he was in his physical body or out of his body, the Bible says God knows, this man was caught up into the third heaven into Paradise. I said, what are you saying, people won't believe you, 'cause even if the dead come back they still won't believe. They have the Law of Moses, the Law of the Prophets. He said, Ian, if they don't believe, don't worry, refer them to me.

There are people that will argue theology with you, don't argue with them, just tell them to talk to Me because I know what took place. He said, if they think it's just a vision, that's alright but I am the One who knows if you rose from the dead and whether I gave you your life back. He said, let them talk to Me about it.

He said, doctors can make mistakes, you could make mistakes; that's right I could be wrong but He said, son, I don't make mistakes. I have called you, I have chosen you, I have appointed you and anointed you to share the love of my Son; the Good News of the Gospel to all these thousands of people. Some of them will listen to what you share and say, Yes, I want to make peace with God, yes, I want to be born again, yes, I want to come out of darkness. I want to know the forgiveness of God and have a clean start. I want to walk in purity, I want to walk in the light of God and be one with Him. I want to know His love.

And He said, son, you can pray with people and they will respond and give their life to Me. He said, that's what you saw, thousands of people that in eternity are going to come through because they've heard what I've done in your life.

I said, God, could I do that with people? He said, that's right; all they have to do is bow in prayer and say, "God, forgive me of my sins, cleanse me of all my sins and if that's you; if you're reading this now, **you** can give your life to God. He can forgive you no matter how evil or how messed up you are, no matter how much drugs or sexual sin you've done, no matter how much filth you've been involved in, He can forgive you. No matter how holy you might think you are, God says, all people have sinned and if you want to pray with me, you can give you life to Jesus.

I'd like you to bow your head and just with me, wherever you are say: God, I ask you to forgive me of all my sins; I ask you to cleanse me and purify me. I believe that Jesus Christ died on that cross and His blood, the blood of His sacrifice, the blood of Jesus Christ will cleanse my spirit as white as snow; I humble myself in prayer and say God have mercy on me, forgive me and cleanse me this day and God as you forgive me, I forgive others that have sinned against me. As you did on the cross, you forgave those who crucified you; God I forgive those who have abused me and wounded me and I give my whole life over to the Lordship of Jesus; I make Him Lord of my life and Savior.

I choose to walk from this day on, in the light of His teaching, the light of His holiness, the light of His Spirit; His Holy Spirit, I invite His Holy Spirit to come in and make Jesus real to join with my spirit to be born again of the Spirit of the Living Christ, Jesus my Lord and Savior; I pray this sincerely from my heart, Amen.

Chapter 2 – A Frequent Flyer

Oden Hetrick made his final trip to Heaven on February 5th, 2001 at the age of seventy-nine. Prior to that, he lived a life devoted to God and documented his frequent 'trips' to the heavenly realms. Here is an interview he did in which he describes some of the things he experienced in his visions.

Interviewer: It is my privilege to introduce you to Reverend Oden Hetrick and his daughter Miss Lois Hetrick. Reverend Oden Hetrick was born on May 21, 1922 in Pennsylvania and when he was twelve years of age, God healed his weak heart. At the age of sixteen, he gave his life to Jesus. Since then, he has set his heart on going to heaven. And after many years of prayer and seeking God, the Lord has blessed him by sending Angels to take him in the Spirit many times to see the City of Heaven. And from time to time through visions, the Lord reminds him of what he's experienced in heaven.

He was married in 1946, graduated in 1951 from Niack Bible College with Bachelor of Theology degree. He worked with a Christian radio and television ministry while raising a son and four daughters. Now, Oden Hetrick and his family work full time in the service of the Lord as an evangelistic team as the gospel singing Hetrick Family.

Oden Hetrick, Lois welcome.

Oden Hetrick: Thank you.

Interviewer: Reverend Hetrick, you've made a trip that we've read about, talked about, sung about, but you people have made this same trip; you've visited heaven. That must be a wonderful experience.

Oden Hetrick: Very much so.

Interviewer: So what we're going to do is talk about your visit, or visits. Not many people have done that.

Oden Hetrick: I don't suppose.

Interviewer: Now you don't look a lot different than most people, how is it that you were chosen to visit heaven?

Oden Hetrick: That's a very good question, I asked the Lord that. I said "Lord, how is it that you give me all these blessings?" And the Lord said to me about the same thing He said to the children of Israel, it's not because there's so many of you, it's not because you're so great, it's just because I love you. Just because I love you. God loves us I guess more than we can understand.

Interviewer: So good looks don't count? (laughing)

Oden Hetrick: It doesn't make any difference.

Interviewer: Intelligence doesn't count?

Oden Hetrick: No. not with God. Just because God loves us.

Interviewer: And because He loves you, He has allowed you to visit heaven. The first visit was about 1952. Since that time, how many times have you visited heaven?

Oden Hetrick: Well I stopped counting at eighty.

Interviewer: At eighty. And when you're there do you enjoy it?

Oden Hetrick: Oh yes. Don't wanna come back. This Earth doesn't look too good anymore.

Interviewer: And each time is new and different?

Oden Hetrick: Oh yes, that's the idea, each time I learn something new.

Interviewer: You see something different?

Oden Hetrick: Yes. And the thing about it is I never forget what I learned the first time. Now I learned a lot that I learned in grade school you know but I never forget what I see when I see heaven.

Interviewer: And you build on each experience?

Oden Hetrick: Yes, that's right.

Interviewer: How did the first visit or how do your visits usually take place?

Oden Hetrick: Well maybe I should explain that the Lord had to open my spiritual eyes first and it was like this. One night ten angels appeared around my bed; now when I opened my eyes they were gone. I couldn't understand that. Then when I shut my eyes to go to sleep again, there they were like before. Well later I learned that was how the Lord opened my spiritual eyes.

Interviewer: By having Angels appear?

Oden Hetrick: Yes. That I could see those Angels. Well then after seeing Angels for a few months, then three of these Angels came and they didn't talk to me, they talked among themselves and said, "Let's take this fellow up and show him around heaven." I can still remember what they said. Of course I didn't feel that I was worthy to go to heaven and I remonstrated with them. I said, "Now look, hold it fellas". But I learned, that when your Angel comes for you, you don't say no. God sent the Angels and they come to take you.

Interviewer: Did you think that would be just a visit or you would stay?

Oden Hetrick: Well, I didn't understand much about at that time, no. I learned later what was going on.

Interviewer: When you made these or make these trips; when we go to heaven what kind of body do we have?

Oden Hetrick: That's an interesting question. I discuss with people about my soul. Looks like me; if my soul would step out of my physical body, it would look just like me. A lot of people when they go from this earth to that heaven; when they die and so forth; the first thing they notice is they are still themselves. You know, I'm still me, I'm still here, I have a body. I can think, I can see, I can smell, taste and touch and that surprises them very much that they can do that. But you see the senses are usually thought of as physical senses but they really belong to the soul and we take these senses with us when we leave this world, we'll still be able to communicate.

Interviewer: We retain the five senses?

Oden Hetrick: Yes, we retain our memory and our senses and our personality.

Interviewer: Physical appearance?

Oden Hetrick: Yes, our physical appearance like we appeared like, but of course it's much more beautiful but...

Interviewer: Describe that beauty. Alight?

Oden Hetrick: Uh, yes, the glorified body, the spirit body, we'll say, the glorified body would be the same; is white as though light is coming from it. We have hair on our hands now but it'll be light. As when in the case of Moses was in Mount Sinai you remember when he came down he had to cover his face because his face shone with the glory of God.

Interviewer: He'd been in the presence of God.

Oden Hetrick: He'd been in the presence of God and I believe it is because the Spirit of God lives in us and shines out through us, that's what makes our bodies appear to be as white.

Interviewer: So we will appear the same, we will be recognizable as ourselves?

Oden Hetrick: Yes, in more ways than one. Now I know you by your name, but I also know you by just talking with you, hearing the tone of your voice and sensing your cheerful spirit. These go to make up you in my mind and that's how we recognize people in heaven;

not just by the shape of my nose or something like that or my hair. (laughs)

Interviewer: So our bodies will look the same, appear the same but it won't be our physical body?

Oden Hetrick: No, there's a difference between the physical; the physical body is just for this Earth; it's just a physical creation, we call it the third dimension. Spiritual bodies are in another dimension.

Interviewer: So it is the soul body?

Oden Hetrick: Yes, the spirit body.

Interviewer: Are we as tall or shorter or is there any difference or could you tell?

Oden Hetrick: I noticed that everybody appeared to be the same size and it looked to me to be about five and a half feet. And me being so tall, it looked funny to me and yet the Angels appeared to be about seven feet tall, the ones that I saw. And then I read in the Bible where Jesus said to the lawyers, who thought they were smart by the way, he said "you can't even add one cubit to your stature". Well that got me to thinking it's only short people up there in heaven and then I learned we can add one cubit to our stature, see, it makes us seven feet tall.

Interviewer: Every one appeared to be the same size? No tall no short.

Oden Hetrick: No, the reason there're short is they take the humble appearance, see, everyone wants to be humble. They can't be any smaller than that so that's the common denominator.

Interviewer: Is approximately five and a half feet.

Oden Hetrick: About that.

Interviewer: Uh, so how do we dress? You have a nice suit on now, Lois has a beautiful skirt and blouse and I think I have a nice suit, recently purchased. Do we get to wear these suits there?

Oden Hetrick: No, uh, in heaven there three different garments we wear. The first one is the garment of humility. It is a soft white garment that fits very neatly and then over top of that we wear the robe of righteousness. These are comparable incidentally to the robes the priest wore when he worshipped; when he served God in the temple. Now this is a long, shining garment. And this is what is usually described by people who have had visions of heaven. And then over top of that, we wear a sleeveless coat, looks like a sleeveless coat and comes down around about just below the knees. And it is set with all kinds of diamonds and rubies and jewels; very beautiful and sparkling; and this is called the garment of praise. And that garment of praise, we put on all these garments, make ourselves seven feet tall and then go into the presence of God to worship.

Interviewer: With all those garments?

Oden Hetrick: All those garments.

Interviewer: What does Heaven look like?

Oden Hetrick: That's a good question and a lot of people want to know that. When God told Moses to make the Tabernacle, He said, "See that you make it according to the pattern I showed you on the Mount." Well that pattern was the city of Heaven, see? And so when Moses made this Tabernacle it had a large outer court and inside of that it had the holy place and inside of that the most holy place. That's the general layout of the whole thing.

Interviewer: Can you describe the outer courts.

Oden Hetrick: The large outer bounds, that could be called suburbs because they are outside of the city walls; outside the city; suburbs. And this is where people first go as I understand it. Whether they die, whether they have a vision or whatever, they go to this place first because they must learn, we must learn that the Spirit of God controls everything in the City of God, see. And so there are no traffic signals because the Spirit of God directs everything. This is how He does it: He puts the thought in our mind, which is: 'Let's go to the river'. And so we say, "Okay, let's go to the river." See, immediate obedience; willing obedience, and it's as though it was our own idea sometimes. Sometimes we'll say, well I'd like to do this and it's the Spirit of God directing us because we are so yielded to the Spirit. Obey the Spirit, you will hear a preacher say; that's the truth; that's where we have to learn to obey the Spirit of God.

Interviewer: I understand that but when we first go to heaven, I'm going to this outer court, the suburbs first there?

Oden Hetrick: Oh it's, it looks very much like the Earth so that the transition as you learn the next lessons will not be too heavy, too strong. And so there are trees, birds, pets, that's where the pets are and flowers and fellowship with people.

Interviewer: Mountains, Lakes?

Oden Hetrick: Mountains, you have very high mountains, lakes, this where the topography is very much like the Earth.

Interviewer: Sounds like a nice place itself.

Oden Hetrick: It is, some people want to stay here but you know we have to grow.

Interviewer: We have described the suburbs of heaven; now the heavenly city itself the New Jerusalem, the second part of this heaven, is how large?

Oden Hetrick: I believe it is actual size as the Bible gives, 12,000 furlongs; now this is just a little bit short of fifteen hundred (1,500) miles. That's a pretty big place.

Interviewer: 1500 miles long?

Oden Hetrick: Right, high and wide and deep; long however you wanna say it.

Interviewer: The great cube of the city.

Oden Hetrick: Cube right, just like the most holy place of Moses' tabernacle.

Interviewer: And there are gates around the city.

Oden Hetrick: Twelve gates. Right and uh the twelve gates, The Apostle John talks about them being shut and being opened and never shut and yet they look shut and he calls them a pearl so to get all these things together; you know a pearl is white, it's a; you can look into a pearl yet you can touch the surface of it; the white isn't on the surface, that's what it look likes.

You approach the gate, you see this light and as you go toward the light you can see into the light and you right through the light into the city.

Interviewer: You're enveloped by the gate.

Oden Hetrick: Right, the gate is never open, it's never shut; you can always just walk into it because that's what John means when he says never shut because you can walk right through this; looks like a pearl.

The wall of the city looks white too and bright. And the gates are very high. Three gates on each side. And as we come close to the city, we can see the three gates and there seems to be decoration around the gates; different colored, not exactly like a rainbow but somehow they are colored. If I would describe them a certain way, the next minute they would be a different way because these things change you know. But over the gates, there's a name, one of the twelve tribes of Israel. Their names are written over top of the gates, one name for each gate. Over top of the eastern gate is the name Isaacher; one of the twelve tribes.

Interviewer: Saint Peter isn't at the gate?

Oden Hetrick: No, that idea of Saint Peter letting us in isn't quite right.

Interviewer: By the time we got that far, we're in.

Oden Hetrick: Right. They know us and the Angels call us by name. And they have a record of us.

Interviewer: They recognize us?

Oden Hetrick: Yes, they recognize us. Angels know us not just by our name, but by our character and by the fact that we're saved by the blood of Jesus and wearing this robe of righteousness. We look very much like the Angels in this nice long white shining garment. Oh, I might mention that inside the gate it looks like a large hallway. You've probably been in churches with large domes and a big hallway, that's kind of what it's like because the gate is two hundred and sixteen (216) feet thick and that makes a nice long hallway. And on the sides of the hallway, are archways like a third of a circle. They're not sharp like this, just like a third of a circle and in those places are what on Earth would be offices and the records are kept. So when we greet the Angel at the gate, he is there to welcome us.

Interviewer: Is he outside the gate?

Oden Hetrick: He's inside the gate, he's inside the gate and he's at the end of the hallway just before you step into the holy part, the holy place of heaven. He's there and he greets you and there could be other Angels there to greet those who are coming in; that's going to be our homecoming; beautiful experience. I mean that's what you look forward to and during the Eastern gate, by the way, the reason you go in at the Eastern gate, is because the throne of God faces that Eastern gate, right.

Interviewer: Now we've talked about, you mentioned Angels; now again you said Angels first took you to heaven; talked among themselves and said they were going to take you to heaven and now we're being greeted by Angels as a homecoming, uh what do Angels look like?

Oden Hetrick: Well, Angels appear to be seven feet tall; they appear always to be seven feet tall because they are sent on errands; when God sends an Angel on an errand, then they take this size of seven feet and they go and do the job. Very friendly beings and they to be, wanna be our servants and serve us. Now the Angels that I saw, did not have wings.

Interviewer: None of the have wings?

Oden Hetrick: Well some of them do, like Seraphims and those who attend God at His throne, the four living creatures like having six wings but those are special beings different from the ordinary, shall we say, if you can say that, from the regular class of Angels.

Interviewer: Is anything ordinary in Heaven?

Oden Hetrick: No, not really. Heaven is a very special place, I try to encourage everybody to go there.

Interviewer: But to go there, we have to get ready here.

Oden Hetrick: We have to get right here, that's right. Get our name written in the Lambs book of life and be ready.

Interviewer: We have now entered the wonderful Eastern gate, through the hall of records, had a homecoming with the Angels, and now what do we see?

Oden Hetrick: The first thing we see is the tree of life. Now I used to think this was one tree but it is a row of trees that contain the fruit alongside of the River of Life. But first I'd like to tell you about a piece of fruit I tasted. It looked sort of like a pear, smooth skin you know and it was juicy. When I took a bite out of it I just couldn't stop the juice from running down my arm and dripping off my elbow, juicy, I thought oh my I'm all stained but there was no stain.

I read another lady, ate the same piece of fruit so I'm pretty sure I was right on that to confirm what I saw you know. Now this fruit grows as John says, different fruit every month and when somebody takes a piece of fruit, another piece appears right away because a lot of people partaking of the fruit and this is where a lot of time is spent in heaven partaking of the fruit.

Interviewer: You say a different fruit every month, it could be a pear one month, an apple...

Oden Hetrick: Yes, different types of fruit and while one fruit is coming ripe, there are flowers on the tree, fragrant flowers, that are going to be in that fruit. And Enoch say this place and he said, "Oh the fragrance." Really terrific you know.

Interviewer: So you said before we have all of our sense of smell, touch; you could smell the blossoms?

Oden Hetrick: Oh yes.

Interviewer: You could taste the fruit.

Oden Hetrick: My mouth is watering.

Interviewer: You see it, you taste it, you smell it, you feel it; the tree of life. And then the river of life.

Oden Hetrick: Yes, just beyond the tree of life is the river of life. Now it's called the crystal river or the river of life whatever you wanna call it. One day my Angel guide said today we're going to step in the river. I said, "Oh but I've got shoes on." And I looked at my feet and I didn't have any shoes on. So I don't think we really wear shoes in heaven. We just like to walk around on the grass. So anyway, we stepped into the river; now it's not cold wet water but it is exhilarating.

Refreshing, perhaps as a boy you stuck your toe in the cold water in the springtime, you know ooohhh so it is very exhilarating. And so we walked into the river, it got deeper and deeper until finally the surface of the river was over the top of our head, we were still breathing and so then I got the understanding, this is the flowing of the Spirit of God; it is a manifestation of the Spirit of God and in heaven, one of the first things we do inside here, is to take the people into this river and there the.., well let me explain it this way; on earth our sins are washed away in Jesus blood. Our souls are made clean in Jesus blood. But when we get to heaven we still remember these things. Even though our sins are washed away.

Interviewer: We remember earthly experiences?

Oden Hetrick: We remember how we were on Earth, you know. And God said these things are going to be wiped away. Well it's bathing in the river that's gonna wipe these memories, these scars, we might call them, scars of sin. Even though the sin is washed away our memory has scars of these things and we keep washing until these scars are washed away from our memory;

and then we can better enjoy heaven. Like I felt when I first went, oh I'm not fit. But this makes us feel fit to enter into the kingdom of heaven and talking about the spirit of God, there are also fountains, I mean beautiful, way up in the air, fall down, sometimes they're caught in basins but my daughter had an experience about this, I think you'd find interesting.

Interviewer: An experience with fountains?

Oden Hetrick: Yes.

Interviewer: Lois, you've also visited heaven and I know you could tell us a lot of things but let's hear about your delightful fountain experience.

Lois Hetrick: Okay, this visit to heaven that I had was the one that I had, when I was sixteen, it was not hard for me to visit heaven because Dad had been telling us ever since we were young of his visits and we were always excited to hear more about heaven.

One day I was at youth camp and after the service we were, a lot of the young people were in the back room praying together. There were a lot of people around me praying, we were all praying out loud and nobody was paying any attention to anyone else; it was at that time that I was praying and praising the Lord and I, I seemed to be able to see around me and I was in a garden, there were um tall trees, tall slender trees that there leaves went all the way down to the ground, there was no trunk that you could see. I was on green grass and directly in front of me and falling over me was a fountain of water. The base of this fountain was clear like crystal, delicately carved like cut glass but you could see right through it, it was pure and clear. The water coming out of it was flowing all the way up and over me but it did not hurt. It was soft and it was warm and yet invigorating, comforting. I stepped out of this water and turned around and there I saw the head and shoulders of Jesus in this water; in this fountain.

And Jesus stepped out of the fountain towards me also; He had His hands out towards me like this. And there were other people in the garden with me; there were six people and Jesus together in this garden. And we sat down right on the grass and we had what we would call lunch or tea. I don't know what we ate, I don't remember.

And after we had tea there we all stood up and, I sensed it my turn, my time to leave, to leave this beautiful place. My back was to a river and I didn't want to go; and I said, "I don't want to go, do I have to go?" And the Lord said to me that, "You must go now but you may return again and again. And I think that anybody who visits heaven doesn't want to come back, they want to go there.

Interviewer: You wanted to stay?

Lois Hetrick: Yes, I did. Incidentally I did visit that place again later and I noticed something that I didn't notice before and that is that the water coming out of the fountain was very loud and rushing and very exciting; like when you see a waterfall, it's really loud.

Interviewer: You talk about the tree of life, and the river of life, Lois about the wonderful fountain experience, now what about the street of gold?

Oden Hetrick: Now this golden street is right next to the Tree of Life. And the Tree of Life is right next to the Crystal River and then the same thing is on the other side; Tree of Life and then Golden Street.

Interviewer: Is it one street that is interconnected or is it a group of streets?

Oden Hetrick: It is uh, that's a rather complicated question; in a way it's connected and in a way it's different. But uh, it, the gold pavement goes a certain distance and then there's grass with flowers around it, the Tree of Life. And then there's another section where you come to the gold again, and that seems to be the base of the river. The bed of the river seems to be gold. And then the other side, the same thing. And this street, and a row of tress, and river, spirals through this holy place; it spirals from the throne of God it comes clear down to the Eastern Gate, and that's where it ends.

So there are five major colors in heaven; gold, red, purple, or violet, the light color, wine tone it might be and blue and green. Those are the major colors of heaven. Now these colors are what make heaven interesting. Let me compare it to a sky. You're used to seeing the sky change colors, you know. The sunset, never two alike; always changing, interesting. So that's what these colors do in heaven, they make colorful sky but mostly it is gold. These colors are more for like decorating the walls of the temple; the other walls around the gates; foundations, these things have their colors in them and these five major colors blend together of course to make other colors.

You might say well, where's orange? I don't know except orange is the color of some flesh, maybe that's why that color is omitted. But then gold is very close to that.

Interviewer: Right, and that's the sky color.

Oden Hetrick: The sky color is usually that color. One time in Florida, we saw the clouds all lit up gold and as they shone down, the leaves in the trees were gold, the ground was gold and the way the light shone from all angles, there were no shadows under the trees. We were sitting in church one time I said; I disturbed the service by saying look at that, just like heaven; the preacher was trying to maintain some composure.

Interviewer: There are no shadows in heaven.

Oden Hetrick: No shadows.

Interviewer: So the light source emanates from everywhere.

Oden Hetrick: Seems to come from everywhere but mainly from the throne of God which we'll be talking about a little later, yes.

Interviewer: We have a river, but you didn't mention swimming; we have a street of gold but you didn't mention walking, what is the mode of transportation?

Oden Hetrick: Good question, uh, the River of Life, people consider themselves swimming in the river and when as we said they bathe in the river to wash the bad memories, it's not, we don't need to wash but they call it bathing. And we do swim in the river, play in the river, it's a park, what it is.

Interviewer: And Lois splashes in the water?

Oden Hetrick: Splashes in the water, yeah and just have a good time there; but now transportation, that's quite a subject.

Mostly, but not mostly I'd say, it is possible to move by the speed of thought. You have to go somewhere and just like that you're there. But there is a mode to move slowly. You have the sensation of moving which in itself is delightful. When you ride down a scenic road, you can look out and see the scenery whereas travelling by thought you wouldn't see that because right away you're there. But to travel, you see, you learn as you travel, oh it's delightful to learn you see. And then you just appear to be floating through space, like we see birds flying through space, seem to float we say. While we don't have any wings we just float through space.

Interviewer: Would that be comparable to walking on air?

Oden Hetrick: Yes, but people don't walk. No, it's not pedestrian, they just move gracefully and uh some people think that's there's chariots and they think of Elijah being caught up in a chariot of fire and horses of fire, you know all that, but that's for demonstration on Earth. In heaven they have little chariots but not all this flamboyance; they don't call attention to themselves. They're more like the Angels, servants; they're just there to serve the saints. And these are, they can be small like two-seater, like in the old days you take your girlfriend for a ride in a two-seater you know or they can be like buses; have a lot of seats. And these vehicles can move on the land or on the river you know or through the sky, any place that; and the Spirit of God moves them.

Interviewer: That was my question, do we direct those vehicles?

Oden Hetrick: No, this comes back to as we discussed, we must be yielded to the Spirit of God and this yielding seems to be difficult on earth for us to learn, but in heaven we'll have to learn this complete yieldedness to the Spirit of God and delight; Jesus said, I delight to do thy will for my Father, for my Lord in my heart.

So we have this delight. The apostle Paul said, if I do this willing I have a reward, see. So heaven is not a place where, oh I'm doing God's will not my will, see. They mistake that by what Jesus said when he had to suffer on the cross. We won't be suffering in heaven, see. We'll be delighting ourselves in these things.

And so these chariots are moved by the Spirit of God to take us where he wants to take us and we just go along for the ride.

Interviewer: So you float for want of a better expression and you have little vehicles, any other mode of transportation?

Oden Hetrick: Now there are other persons who've visited and they talk about different type of chariots which could be but I mean I can't say what I don't know.

Interviewer: You didn't see.

Oden Hetrick: I didn't, no, that's what I understand.

Interviewer: Is time kept in heaven? Are there days, weeks, months, years?

Oden Hetrick: Heaven is a very interesting place, there's nothing monotonous including the passage of time on earth, see. Not it, on Earth you sense the passing of time, the clock ticks, you know, the sun goes over the horizon and you sense the passing of time, you don't sense the passing of time but there are different periods of time. There's a time when the sky is bright and this we call day and then there's a time when the sky is not so bright. Old folks had a name for it, 'gloaming' in the evening time; some folks think this is when God walked with Adam and Eve in the garden, at the cool of evening, see.

It's a time when activity seems to slow down. And this day and night so they call it, no night in heaven but light and less light; hard to put it in English you know; uh it makes a twenty-four hour period.

Interviewer: You put it in human...

Oden Hetrick: Yes, same as we have on Earth.

Interviewer: Twenty-four hour period?

Oden Hetrick: Yes, and then the daylight time would go in seven day lengths so then you have the week and then at the end of the week there's a special day set aside for special worship services in God's presence.

Interviewer: What about communication, are there any language barriers in heaven?

Oden Hetrick: I suppose that's an important question people would like to know. We think of communicating by thoughts on Earth like sometimes among our family, if somebody's out somewhere and the phones rings we say oh that's David, because we know; well that's one way that we communicate. I mean we can know what the other person is thinking, uh, but speaking of languages there, you know Adam and Eve only spoke one language but somewhere along the line down there about the Tower of Babel, you know, overnight God changed the languages. And the next morning everybody spoke a different language and they didn't understand each other and so that's been with us down through the ages and as I understand it God is going to bring this all again; it might be expressed in the words there of Paul, bringing everything together in one in Christ Jesus; which would include languages. One language, see, coming into one language.

Interviewer: Jesus said in my Father's house are many mansions and I go to prepare you one. I want you to tell me about mansions in heaven.

Oden Hetrick: Very good subject. As I approach my mansion which I am going to call my country mansion, there's a Rose arbor in front of it, with a heart shaped trellis. You go through this heart shaped trellis, lovely row of flowers on this side. I don't know what they are but someone told me they were Chrysanthemums; I described them for him and he said they must be Chrysanthemums. And the mansion itself sits on about ten acres, large place. And then we go into the vestibule; large round, about twenty feet round.

Interviewer: Inside the front door?

Oden Hetrick: Inside the front door, yes, when you enter through the front door. So as you step in this vestibule, to the right is a door, and in that door is the banquet room and to the left is a door, and in that door is the fellowship hall or the living room as would say on Earth. And then in front of you is a spiral stairway that goes up to the other floors, then on the second floor there is a huge balcony that overlooks the garden so that you can be up on a balcony and look down into the garden and see what's growing down there. The second is, music room, piano, I play a guitar so I have a guitar.

Interviewer: Any special kind?

Oden Hetrick: Well yes, very special, it is inlaid with white mother-of-pearl; like the gates of the city we talked about; very beautiful. Let's talk about a banquet now in the banquet room. We gather in this room, we gather our friends, like my father may want to be his brothers and sisters but there's sometimes when I want my father with me and his children, see, plus other friends we'd gather around. Now I sit at the servant end of the table and Jesus sits at the head of the table.

Interviewer: Jesus is at your banquet?

Oden Hetrick: Jesus comes to the banquet, yes, he did on Earth, He does in heaven and we think of Jesus as standing at God's right hand but you see Jesus is able to appear anyplace He wants to. He's not just in my banquet, but there's other banquets and he can appear also in all those other banquets at the same time. The word omnipresent, it really means what it says. We think of the Spirit of God being Omnipresent because we can't see it. And we think something that we see can't be omnipresent but that's not the case. Even though we can see Jesus in heaven, He is still omnipresent, He can be any place He wants to be.

Now we're not omnipresent, we're only one place at a time but that's now the case with Jesus.

Interviewer: In heaven we are in one place but Jesus can be at your banquet, my banquet, Lois' picnic, brother Joe's party.

Oden Hetrick: Yes, and at the same time standing at the right hand of God. And then the people sit around the sides. And then the person who is serving comes in and directs what is to serve and they go back out again. And they bring in a platter. Now as we said before, most things in heaven are gold but this is a silver platter, I don't know why, I just noticed it was a silver platter. It's oval shaped like a platter usually is and on this platter is little things that look like bon-bons, with food, and I don't know if you ever tasted Almond Butter; but it's like Almond Butter and then they flavor it with dried fruit and very tasty.

And so, it's not piled high, just neatly put on a tray, the food. And as it's passed around, each person takes a piece, passes it to the next person and when one piece is taken, another piece appears in its place! You know, something like the five loaves and two fishes.

Interviewer: It never ran out.

Oden Hetrick: It never ran out, just kept passing them out as it went around the table. Well I forget to mention there's little angelic creatures something that makes the music. You don't put your cassette in a boom-box and press the button.

Interviewer: No stereos?

Oden Hetrick: No stereos, just little angels that make this music.

Interviewer: While you're eating or all the time?

Oden Hetrick: Well especially at the banquet, I could see them. I was wondering where the music was coming from and I could see them just singing. There seemed to be instruments but I couldn't see where that was coming from.

Now there are intimacies in heaven, let explain this; we were talking about the Spirit of God living in us you know. People say well what, how does the Spirit of God live in us? Let me say this, my soul is in my body, just like I put my hand in a glove. The glove's dead until I put my hand in it, as soon as I put my hand in it, it comes to life. So my soul looks like my body, fits in my body and it gives my soul life, see when my soul departs, my body lifeless.

When Dives was in hell looking at Abrahams bosom, he saw Lazarus, Dives had fingers, he had a memory, he recognized him, even though his body was in the grave, see, very recognizable. So the Spirit of God, the same way, He fits in our body like a hand in a glove. And He gives us spiritual life, our soul gives us physical life, see, but the Spirit gives us Spiritual life. That is an intimacy.

Interviewer: God living in us.

Oden Hetrick: God living in us, that is an intimacy. As the apostle Paul says, "Christ in us and we in Christ". That is an intimacy.

Interviewer: That's what we have here on Earth but in heaven it's to a greater degree.

Oden Hetrick: Yes, but we learn that intimacy here, the kind of intimacies that are in heaven, we learn them here, see. Let's explain it this way; you know when Adam and Eve were in the garden, when God first made this creation, he made a paradise, he made a man and lady and he had fellowship with them. Now that's interesting that's the way God made it. And He said it's good; when He made the man and lady, he not only said it's good, He blessed it, yes He blessed it.

Now coming around full circle to heaven, here we have paradise again, we have the man and the lady again in fellowship with God. Now that's as clear as I can make it.

Interviewer: So as it began before the fall, so shall it be in the end.

Oden Hetrick: This is the way God wanted it, if He had wanted it some other way, He would have done it some other way. As He said about what you quoted a while ago; "if it were not so, I would have told you" like the mansions in heaven, see. So if He had wanted it otherwise, He would have made it otherwise.

I think by now, people may be wondering, are there ladies in heaven? I've heard some people say no, there's just going to be men in heaven, we're all going to be men in heaven; but I asked a lady one time if she was going to heaven and she said, "I sure am".

Interviewer: (laughs) And she didn't intend to become a man,

Oden Hetrick: That's right, she didn't intend to become a man, she intended to become a lady.

Interviewer; Jesus said there is no marriage in heaven yet you talk about companionship. How do you explain marriage and companionship in heavens light?

Oden Hetrick: That's a good question, I'm going to do the best I can to answer that. You're quoting to me from Luke chapter 20, where Jesus said, "those who are counted worthy to obtain the resurrection, do not marry or are given in marriage". Now that Greek word there means they do not reproduce, see. Jesus did not say, there's no companionship, He said, there's no reproduction. That word from there means reproduce in the physical sense.

See on Earth, physical bodies die and have got to be replenished but in heaven it's not so. But let's go back to the Garden of Eden, this might help to clear things up. You see when God first created this world, this world that you and I live in, He put two lovers in paradise and had fellowship with them. It's like this, when God made Eve, it was not as though He made another apple, if you'll pardon the apple expression. It was as though he cut the first apple in half, the first apple being Adam. He took Adam and He cut, that's what sex means, to divide, see. And so in dividing like that, He divided them not just physically, male and female, He divided them emotionally, spiritually, socially, and in all of these ways.

So that the feminine being has her characteristics and the masculine being has his characteristics but in Adam, they were male and female. It was a feminine being living in a female body and a masculine being living in a male body. Now, when we get to heaven, we'll still be masculine and feminine but no more male and female.

The Song of Solomon, he talks about perfection in relationship to your spouse, making you perfect, see. Now people think they're going to choose their own companion on Earth; this fella said when he went to church camp, he said, "Lord, show me who she is and let me chase her." Well, that's not exactly – see Adam didn't choose Eve.

Interviewer: They were made for each other.

Oden Hetrick: God, made them for each other and neither of them had anything to say in the whole thing. It was God's idea, we can't save ourselves, God has to wash away our sins. When it comes time to leave this world, we can't do it. We don't decide when, we don't decide – we can't take ourselves up to heaven, see. God has to take us.

So when it comes to deciding the eternal state and our companion there in heaven, it's totally up to God. Well, I suppose we could refer to chapter five of Ephesians, there Paul is talking about the husband and the wife, and he's talking about Christ and the bride the church. And after he talks about this union a while, saying they should respect each and so forth, when he gets down to the end he says, it's a great mystery. And I suppose it's going to remain a mystery until we get to heaven and we find out about the details.

What I do know is that there's companionship in heaven.

Interviewer: Notwithstanding the humanness of it, I'm pretty happen with my marriage here and I believe there are a lot of couples who are happily married. When they get to heaven, these couples, will they remain with their Earth-mate? Or will they get different companions.

Oden Hetrick: No, it's very likely, there are a lot of people who are happily married, about 85% according to my research. And it's my understanding God's not going to break up a good thing; it's very likely the companionship will remain, a delightful companionship will remain. But for those 15% who are unhappily married, I do have to say that God has the answers. And He's gonna make it right when he gets to heaven. And you know also this relationship is like Christ and His bride the church. Now that's a very sacred relationship. We don't think of Christ and His bride the church being man and wife in heaven in the sense that they are on

Earth but Revelation 19 does call the church the bride of Christ; even His wife it says.

But that's not the proper meaning there, it means He's a companion. We are Jesus' companion, we have fellowship with Jesus, we have intimacies with Jesus. Let me give you another illustration. You see in the Garden of Eden, when Eve partook of the forbidden fruit, Adam knew that if he partook, he'd die. But he was willing to partake of that forbidden fruit to be with his companion.

Now you see she was — she is part of him, I mean she was taken from his side, I think it was the right side, she was taken from his side as a curved rib so she's very much a part of him.

Interviewer: He didn't want to be separated.

Oden Hetrick: He did not want to be separated from Eve, I mean, I think the love there that we don't understand, like he did, he just couldn't be separated. Well it's the same way with Christ I believe you because when He hung on the cross there and that soldier pierced his side and that is where the blood flowed out of his side. And if we understand the scripture correctly, it's the blood of Jesus that washes our sins away and makes us part of the bride of Christ. And Jesus – I mean when you give blood for somebody, as He said, greater love has no man.

Interviewer: He laid down His life.

Oden Hetrick: He laid down his life.

Interviewer: So Jesus did not want to be separated from us and was willing to die for us just as Adam did not want to be separated from Eve.

Oden Hetrick: Right, right.

Interviewer: And so fellowship here on Earth with Jesus is so vital, it must be in heaven even more vital and wonderful. You've met Jesus in heaven?

Oden Hetrick: Oh yes.

Interviewer: Can you describe that meeting or those meetings?

Oden Hetrick: Well let's start with the first one okay. I was praying and fasting at the time and I really wanted to know what God wanted me to do for my life, "What do you want me to do Lord, here I am." And then I, I saw Jesus and he was tall and of course like Daniel I just fell down on my face no breath left in me.

Interviewer: Were you frightened?

Oden Hetrick: No, I wasn't afraid, I was overcome you might say, awestruck but I wanted to do something. So I fell, I just put my arms around his ankles and my head was like this to the side of his ankle and I thought I was crying but I don't know if I was or not. But I was really emotionally stirred up you know and then I saw a little tear come out of my right eye, I thought it was a tear. And it dropped like it was going down in a canyon, and I saw it going down and then I heard the voice of Jesus, He said, "That's how much you love me."

Interviewer: That one drop?

Oden Hetrick: That really shook me up, I said "I thought I loved you move than that Lord". He said, "You have things to learn about love."

Interviewer: And that was your first meeting?

Oden Hetrick: Right, we don't have the right meaning of love on Earth. We've got to learn God's love. And later, I don't know where that took place, I couldn't place it where it was but later I got to talking to Jesus in heaven about some serious things, see, about companions and companionship. And like most people, that's an interesting subject, see. God is our deepest need but a companion is our deepest desire.

Interviewer: Aha, good description.

Oden Hetrick: And I wanted to know about companionship and so the Lord showed me this very beautiful creature, very beautiful lady, very beautiful feminine being and He said "What do you think about her?" I said, "Oh boy, she's really something." He said, "Would you like to have a companion like that?" I said, "Oh boy, that would be my heart's desire." I said, "I don't have a companion, she's not my companion" see. He said, "Now you understand how I'd like to be with my companion. Oh, that really made it plain to me. Jesus wants to be with His bride the church. That's precious to me. Really one of the highlights of my visits to heaven.

Interviewer: So the purpose of heaven is for us to be with Christ.

Oden Hetrick: Exactly right. I couldn't explain it better myself. To fellowship with Jesus, right.

Interviewer: And meet our deepest needs.

Oden Hetrick: It will. Yes, it'll meet our deepest need. And when He finally gets this companionship straightened out, we understand how things are, we meet our deepest desire. And I always tell people, I encourage them to go to heaven, I always tell them, "If you're not satisfied, you can punch me right on the nose!" It wouldn't hurt anyway if they did, see. But I know they'll be satisfied. I just know people will be happy to be with Jesus.

Interviewer: Well, I suppose there's a question on a lot of people's minds, if they are going to be bore in heaven?

Oden Hetrick: I saw a picture one time, of a fella twirling his halo around his finger.

Interviewer: Nothing else to do?

Oden Hetrick: Like there's nothing to do in heaven, oh no. That is not the truth at all. If all we did was enjoy the fellowship of our common companions and enjoy the presence of Jesus, if that's all we did, let me tell you it would be outta sight.

Interviewer: And will there be companionship with our loved ones who have gone on?

Oden Hetrick: Oh yes, right, our relatives, loved ones and even those we haven't met yet. When we meet them, it's gonna be like an old friend. Being in evangelistic work, you when you meet new Christians, they don't seem strange at all; it seems like you've known them; brothers and sisters in the Lord. It's a love with which we love everybody, and it's the love which carries you along in heaven.

Interviewer: The Bible talks about us laying up treasures in heaven, as opposed to here on Earth where moth and rust do corrupt; in heaven did you see any evidence of 'treasures'.

Oden Hetrick: Yes, I did. In my mansion one day, I went down to the basement; now when we think of a basement, we think of a place not desirable, you can't tell it's a real nice place to be.

Interviewer: Like a rumpus room?

Oden Hetrick: Yeah or like a family room, you know. So I noticed bins of Jewels about two feet wide and about four feet deep; I don't know how deep they were this way, I don't know about two or three feet deep; and different colored jewels in the bins, they were separated you, diamonds, sapphires; my favorite sapphires, my favorite color is blue. I noticed all these bins of jewels, so I ran over to them and I dipped into the rubies, the red ones, I said my favorite color is blue didn't I; I dipped into the red ones first, I picked them up like this and let them dribble down through my fingers; just look at that.

My Angel guide was there showing me these things; that's what you get and the bible says if you even give a cup of cold water in the name of a disciple, you get a big reward in heaven. The smallest thing you do gets a large reward in heaven.

Interviewer: And you're rewarded in jewels or that's one of the rewards?

Oden Hetrick: That's one of the ways you would. Girls like jewels better than fellas do but I do like jewels. As I saw those jewels for the first time and was playing with them, my Angel guide said, "Do you like those? And

I said, "Oh they're pretty." But my Angel guide said, "They can't love you in return."

A real lesson.

Interviewer: The most important thing is not ...

Oden Hetrick: Right, the most important thing is fellowship. Love and fellowship. You love somebody and they love you back in return; because jewels can't do that, all they can do is look pretty. The lesson of the jewels; but we must remember that God is in charge of all these things; He even tells Jesus what to do and when God tells Jesus something to do, to obey His Father is His extreme delight, see.

So Jesus has jobs for us to do, little things for us to do and they may be going to the outer environs to comfort a soul who just does not understand the glories of heaven.

Interviewer: The outer environs is the first place you described.

Oden Hetrick: The first place we described, yes.

Interviewer: It looks so much like Earth, beautiful place.

Oden Hetrick: Right, when an Angel, when a child on Earth dies and God sends an Angel to bring that child home, that angel is invincible; he will stop at nothing until his job is finished and while he is doing that job he has extreme delight in obeying God. When God tells us to do something, we obey that; extreme delight.

Interviewer: Now there's another place, the most Holy place, and has several names; I would like you to tell us those names and describe this place.

Oden Hetrick: Alright, you've already given us one name, it's also called the Father's presence. As the scripture tells us in the psalms at His right hand and in His presence is fullness of joy. And also the Temple of Heaven and maybe we should take it like that, the Temple of Heaven. It's large round structure about three hundred miles across and about eight hundred miles high.

Interviewer: This is in the center?

Oden Hetrick: In the center of the four square city. And some folks wonder how they can see three hundred miles and I ask them if they were ever a lover on a park bench they never worried about the moon being 250,000 miles away. They could see it, no problem with the distance in heaven.

Now outside of this wall is the garden of fountains, that's what Lois was talking about yes, those three gardens where fountains of waters come up and we'll be talking more about that later. Then this wall is about fifteen miles thick; it's a big place. Inside of this wall, are a lot of rooms, a lot of activities going on in here. One of those is a temple of instruction where the children are taught and they have Angels who instruct them and as we said a while ago, the Angels bring the children up to heaven and this is where they take them; to the Temple of Instruction.

As Jesus said, talking about children, their angels do always behold the face of my Father in heaven, that's what He was talking about; their instructor Angels can see the face of God.

Lois Hetrick: Were these children little children that died and went to heaven?

Oden Hetrick: Yes, they died in childbirth, they died by accident or they were aborted; whatever the case was with children, they are taken there. And then there are also rooms which we'll call theatres for lack of a better term because the one wall is where the picture; it's sort of like a movie cinema or sort of like a TV; and yet it's like a stage because it's three dimensional but you know it's not real actors because one of the scenes we see there is actually the life of Christ. And we see what happened in the life of Christ.

Interviewer: So the children see.

Oden Hetrick: The children see as part of their instruction. And they see how Jesus died on the cross and this really breaks them up to see Him hanging there on the cross. You see as spirit beings, they can see the demons that were hovering around the cross which the people on earth didn't see and they see this and of course that breaks them up.

Also every saint that goes to heaven is required to see this because after all, Jesus dying on the cross is the reason we are here.

Interviewer: So there is a feeling of remorse sometimes or sadness in heaven?

Oden Hetrick: Yes, strange as it may seem, it's required for our training, required for our training. We must see that scene. Also there is a videotape shall we say, a video cassette of your life and my life.

Interviewer: So that's how the record's kept?

Oden Hetrick: That's one way the records are kept. There's one way in books and writing you know but others are in actual visual sights they can see and hear their life. Now that's enough to make somebody behave isn't it?

Interviewer: Certainly.

Lois Hetrick: The bad parts are cut out though aren't they?

Oden Hetrick: When Jesus forgives our sins, of course, He really washes them away, no trace so that when you look at your life again those areas that would have been sins are cut out; when we're save you know, probably from then on, you can see your life and see what you did on Earth. That's one of the things that takes place in there.

Many other rooms, many other places but this wall only has three gates; a north a south and east. There's none on the west; we'll describe that later why that is. But we going to enter in at the gate that's to the east, we like the Eastern gate because as we said before the throne of God faces the east, right. So we go in to this part and it's huge but the activity takes place in the walls. A lot of activity, there's also chambers. We talked about the country mansions, this is the city mansion.

Interviewer: We have another mansion.

Oden Hetrick: Yes, a city mansion. One day the Spirit of God said to me, "Today I'm going to show you something." And I knew it was going to be something grand, I said "Oh, I'm afraid". And the Spirit of God said, "It's okay". So a little later, the Spirit of God came back and said, "Now I really want you to see this". I said, "Yes, but I'm still afraid". Well, alright.

And then the Spirit of God came the third time, this time we're going so I thought okay, I knew enough not to argue.

Lois Hetrick: When your Angel calls you go.

Oden Hetrick: When your angel calls you go but the Spirit of God seemed to be very patient with me and this touched me; the Spirit of God is patient with us. So the place I went was beyond description. Suppose I were to tell you that a flower stem looks like a plastic drinking straw, I mean it doesn't move you does it? The petals made of diamonds, fourteens inches long which tapered out to a sharp point and I looked around and everything was made of Crystal but the light I told you about the colors, reflecting off these, gave different reflections of color; everything beautiful.

Interviewer: This is inside the city mansion?

Oden Hetrick: This is inside my city mansion which is in Ezekial called a chamber. And then I saw two creatures, crystal clear, a masculine being and a feminine being and I oh, but then I realized they didn't see me and I relaxed a little bit and I said, "Spirit of God I don't belong here, would you please take me out of this place". "After you learn your lesson, I'll take you away", so I stuck with it. And I heard beautiful music, I looked around, I couldn't see any musical instruments, nothing I could recognize as a musical instrument. And I tried to follow the sound and I came to a little brook, a little streamlet, beautiful water, sparkling blue and I said it has to be coming from there.

I walked over and I looked down into that stream there and I saw what were rows of jewels and they were positioned so that as the water fell over them, they made music. You see like a music box like doing, doing, that's the principle. I was flabbergasted.

Interviewer: Like a wind chime, only it's a water chime.

Oden Hetrick: Wind chime, yeah right, that's the idea.

Interviewer: This is within your chamber?

Oden Hetrick: This is within my chamber, what I later understood to be my chamber, I didn't know at the time what it was, I had no idea, see. But then these two being that I saw, they looked at me, boy did I feel terrible. See the beautiful light could shine right through them and make them beautiful but here I was this opaque, putrid, you know Isaiah said, "Lord I am not fit to be in this place".

And an Angel said wait, wait I'll get a coal of fire and touch it to your lips and purified his lips. And that was the way I felt, I really felt terrible in that place. But later on I found out that was my mansion, see.

Let's go to the front of the mansion to the area that looks out over what we described as the most place. The place in front of God's throne. The front of it is like a big window, but there's no window there, you can step right out. Outside is a rainbow pathway. It's sort of called a spiral, it spirals up. You find this description also in Ezekial about the temple. And looking out you see God on his throne.

Interviewer: From your chambers, you can see God.

Oden Hetrick: Yes. From all the chambers you can look out and see God. Now in the front of the chamber, in what we call the front room, there's, the best I can describe it is a bean bag. I'm glad somebody invented bean bags so I can describe this. See, because you just fall in it and it takes your shape. And there you can just relax and observe the face of God. And the walls have these beautiful green and blue and wine toned tints in them and cloud-like it can change; like wallpaper pattern you know; very beautiful.

But let's go out now, and let's pretend we're in the throne of God, standing with God on the throne alright. We look back at the mansion and we see that there is a whole row of mansions, chamber mansions and they reach about two thirds of the way around so that God on His throne can sit and look at all the people who are in the mansions; companions in each chamber. Here we are back again, two companions, paradise, and presence of God.

Lois Etrick: Not only are there 144,000 chambers in one row but there are 144,000 thousand rows.

Oden Hetrick: Now a chamber is about, now this is cubits measure, but in feet, it would be about fifteen feet high and about twenty-five feet wide. That's about the size of this chamber as you're looking at it, see.

Now the throne of God as we said, can be seen by looking out at the mansions, people looking at God's face and God's throne, He looks and sees the chambers. In front of the throne is a large oval area, I'd say two hundred miles; I'm estimating. Two hundred miles long and about seventy five miles wide. Now this is made out of sapphire jewels. I found this also in Ezekial, describing the sapphires underneath the throne of God and it's called a sea because it's blue and because it's shiny. It's called glass because it's actually made of sapphires that represent glass, so that's the term 'sea of glass'. In other words it's not water; it's not the flowing of the Spirit of God, it's a rather solid place to stand.

Interviewer: Is it like a reflecting pool? Does it reflect anything?

Oden Hetrick: It would reflect the light of God, yes. However it doesn't appear to reflect too much light, this appears before God's throne. It's like a moving platform, it can be moved away for other activities. But here's a place where the saints of God appear before god's throne and the prophets, I saw one time the prophets before God's throne and they were talking to God and I saw the martyrs who were saying, "How long o Lord, how long?". All these things making me believe that Jesus was coming soon.

Now one time I was concerned about Jesus receiving something in exchange for dying on the cross for us because the Bible does tell us that He'll see the travail of His soul and He'll be satisfied in Isaiah 53 I believe it is. And so I was allowed to see something in this center, most holy place. It was about, I don't know the number, thousands of saints I would say were gathered in formation; now of course they were dressed in their garments of praise.

Interviewer: With the jewels on them?

Oden Hetrick: Right, and they formed themselves into a cup. Regular cup, everyday, ordinary cup and it seemed to have a base on it and they sparkled, the light of God did sparkle off of their garments and this was called 'the cup of love for Jesus' because these saints, it was their way of expressing their love for Jesus.

Lois Hetrick: and it turned around as they prayed.

Oden Hetrick: Yes, you know how the Earth turns on its axis? There's a Greek word that means 'praise to God'. So this cup of love as it turns, is praising God, see. And then the saints are raising their hands and the cup you see the motion, you see their hands moving in unison. It's just very beautiful thing to see; stand back and see it. It was also a beautiful activity, it's called an activity in the holy place; it's an activity of worship.

Now this cup of love, it's presenting love to Jesus; it makes up to him something that He suffered because in the Garden of Gethsemane, you remember He prayed, "My Father if it's possible, let this cup pass from me…".

Interviewer: The cup of suffering.

Oden Hetrick: The cup of suffering; so see He described it as a cup. And He said, "Nevertheless, not as I will, but as thou will", and of course if He hadn't died for us, we couldn't be Christians.

Interviewer: We couldn't fellowship with Him there.

Oden Hetrick: No, right, we wouldn't be able to fellowship with Him. But that suffering, of course Jesus paid, the Bible says He paid something. And so in this cup, He's receiving it back again. He was buying the love of saints.

Lois Hetrick: He shall see the travail of His soul and He shall be satisfied.

Oden Hetrick: Isaiah, He shall see the travail of His soul and shall be satisfied.

Interviewer: This is His satisfaction.

Oden Hetrick: That is when He receives satisfaction with the love of the saints He died to redeem. Beautiful story.

Interviewer: It is. You talked about the River of Life, all things life proceed from God, is that where this river begins?

Oden Hetrick: That's right, that's right, the light comes from the throne of God, shines down through the city and also the river of life which as we discussed before is actually the flowing of the Spirit of God. It comes from the throne of God and then it flows through the mansions. It's that little river we talked, that little creek, stream.

Interviewer: That how it starts out a little stream?

Oden Hetrick: It goes through the mansions, each mansion right; down through all the mansions, and then when it gets to the bottom, it is, it comes up in the fountains, alright. And then it falls down the basins and is collected, is gathered together and flows out into a river which is rather small at the beginning. And the further it flows, the bigger it becomes.

Interviewer: So the fountain that Lois experienced is part of the river of God?

Oden Hetrick: Yes, she was at the garden of fountains; now we know where she was.

Lois Hetrick: And this river flows in twelve circles through the holy place.

Oden Hetrick: Right, and then it flows out of the Eastern gate and it flows down to earth and we don't see it here because we can't see spiritual things.

Interviewer: This is the love of God in our hearts?

Oden Hetrick: Right, but we know it because we can feel the love of God; the love of God is shed abroad in our hearts by the Holy Spirit; that's the way the Bible says it; and we know it when that happens.

Interviewer: Reverend Hetrick, you've told us a lot about heaven, you seem to know a lot about heaven.

Oden Hetrick: Well, sure that's because I've been there a lot of times.

Interviewer: You've made a lot of visits so that means, you didn't learn it all the first visit?

Oden Hetrick: That's right, you don't get it all at one time.

Interviewer: You feel there's more to learn?

Oden Hetrick: Oh yes, yes, I believe so. This idea that when we get to heaven we're gonna know it all, that's not quite right.

Interviewer: Does our knowledge come by just observing or from classes or running experiences.

Oden Hetrick: Different ways yes, by classes, by observing, talking to others who know something they want to tell you; people who have been in heaven a little longer that we have perhaps. All of these different ways we increase our knowledge. 1st Corinthians also says prophecy shall cease; in heaven you don't need any prophecy, see.

Interviewer: That's the culmination of all prophecy.

Oden Hetrick: Right, that's when everything is going to be fulfilled and perfect. But it does not mean that we are going to have all knowledge at one time. Even after we get to heaven, as much time as we spent on Earth reading the bible, we're still gonna be able to learn when we get to heaven. But it's a good thing to do as much as you can here, you know.

Interviewer: In preparation?

Oden Hetrick: In preparation, because we can't be rewarded for something that we do up there. We're rewarded for our works on Earth.

Different spheres of existence, in other words, the Apostle Paul really suffered in the service of God and a person who just lives a normal life and didn't care about serving God, he expect to go to heaven and be like the Apostle Paul. I mean the Apostle Paul explained it himself this way; there's different glories, like the brightness of the moon, the brightness of the stars, the brightness of the sun, he said so is also those who are resurrected from the dead. There are different glories. And by different glory, it means to shine; they actually shine brighter so that those people on the outer environs could not behold a being, for instance, from the most holy place, a person who goes into the most holy place, he'd be very bright to appear to those people.

Interviewer: Or can a person who now exists in the outer environs, can that person learn more to increase his stature to enter into another place with God there?

Oden Hetrick: Yes, as they increase and as they learn but there's some barrier they can't go beyond, I believe it's the fact that they have no rewards because they didn't do any work. Now everybody gets a golden crown, yes, that's the sign of eternal life; a golden crown and they're all golden. That's one thing I remember, I thought maybe some were silver but they're all golden, even Jesus' crown is golden in heaven, yes. But they don't have like the bins of jewels to give gifts to other people and then as they increase in stature, in glory, they come in and live in the holy place, see, the biggest place that there is outside the environs, when you're inside the city; this is a big place.

And then they increase in glory, the go into the *most* holy place. So a person who resides in a most holy place, spends most of his time there. Person who resides in the holy place will spend most of their time there. Now they do go back and forth, see. But a person with more glory, more brightness, spends more time in the presence of God.

Interviewer: So to achieve eternal life, we accept Jesus Christ as our personal savior, we're washed in the blood of the Lamb. To achieve rewards in heaven, we do works for God here.

Oden Hetrick: Right, we must serve the Lord here. If we don't, we cannot make up for it, I repeat, we cannot make up for it in heaven, no sir.

Interviewer: You can't say God I meant to do more.

Oden Hetrick: Right, intentions will not count. No can't do that, the work has to be done here. Jesus said, "Behold I come quickly and my reward is with me to render to every person according to their work". That's Revelation 21:12, every person according to their work, right.

Lois Hetrick: And no matter what each person gets, each person is completely happy and there's a lot of laughter and happy fellowship in heaven. Everyone is happy with what they received.

Oden Hetrick: I forgot to mention that we were by the Tree of Life and the Crystal River it seemed, yes, everybody is laughing. It's a hilarious place pardon the expression, really, it's just people are always enjoying themselves. Just everything is perfect and beautiful and the more we enjoy ourselves, the more our Creator enjoys Himself. He didn't make us to be robots, He gave us a willpower and when we say God I love you because I want to, God accepts that, see. If we say, God I don't want to love you, we have to suffer the consequences of course, but if we say God I want to love you; that's what He wants.

There is an interesting part here, when God made man, He used what I call the cubit system. The cubit system measures man six measurements like one-finger, two-palm, three-span, four-foot, five-cubit and six-fathom. So man has six measurements.

Interviewer: Fathom is from head to toe.

Oden Hetrick: Right. And he was created on the sixth day of creation so man's number is six. It's nothing to be upset about, that's a fact, that's our number. Nothing to be excited about, right. But the number of heaven is twelve, see you have twelve gates, twelve Angels, twelve thousand furlongs and twelve foundations so these numbers are reference to the city of Heaven.

It so happens that in the cubit system, man, the number of man six, fits perfectly into the cubit system; the number twelve fits perfectly into the cubit system because God made both. And so God made man for the city, he made the city for man. And it is important for us human creatures to know it was God's intention; He built a beautiful city for us to go to. And we should by all means press on as the Apostle Paul did; press toward the mark for the prize of the upward calling of God, that beautiful place.

Interviewer: It was God's intention that we live with Him.

Oden Hetrick: It is God's intention that we live with Him and He has made it beautiful. The problem on this Earth is that we are tempted by the forces of evil and God will not violate our willpower. If we don't want to go, we won't go. We must want to, but here's God pleading with us; Jesus gave His life, He said greater love has no man yet some of us decide not to go; it grieves God's heart.

But those who do decide to go will be pleasing in God's sight and let me tell you, there's a song that says, tell your troubles to Jesus but I tell the people that we sing to; you talk to Jesus when you're happy and watch Him make you happy.

Lois Hetrick: Love the Lord with all of your heart, soul, mind and strength.

Interviewer: Reverend Hetrick you have shared with me and our listeners the joys of heaven, I'm excited and I know they are too. In conclusion are there any other thoughts you would like to share with our friends?

Oden Hetrick: Yes, I would. Friends, I've done my best to tell you the joys of heaven and I'm going there myself, I'm planning on it. And I know that the only way to go there is to accept Jesus as savior and Lord and follow Him and with all my heart seek after Jesus.

We know that by looking at the signs of the times that Jesus is coming soon. Sure I know, I've heard this all my life Jesus is coming soon. But all you have to do is look at the newspaper, watch the news and you know that something has to happen soon. God has got to step in soon and do something. Now, I want you to be ready. I want you to know Jesus as your savior, you must do this in order to be ready. Would you meet me in heaven? I'd like to see you there, yes I would.

Interviewer: As God made the division between darkness and light there is a heaven and there is a hell and we must have a definite, unwavering faith in Christ and a strong hope of heaven. Matthew 13 verse 44 states, "The kingdom of heaven is like a treasure hidden in a field, which a man found and hid and from joy over it, he goes and sells all that he has and buys that field".

We have a glorious opportunity of investing our complete hope in the treasure of heaven. John 2 verse fifteen says, "Don not love the world nor the things in the world. If anyone loves the world, the love of the Father is not in him. But some believers argue that placing too much hope in heaven will result in a sort of escape from this world; a fantasy that perhaps would not be healthy.

Perhaps so heavenly minded that they are no earthly good. But E.M. bounds once so beautifully wrote, the best citizen of heaven is the best citizen of earth. You are a child of God and so being you overcome the world. We are partakers of Christ's victory and triumph over sin and death. We are not going to perish in Jesus but will find a new beginning of everlasting joy and happiness; so seek your rightful heritage; fight the good fight; labor for heaven and its imperishable riches and we'll all meet in heaven. Amen.

Chapter 3 – Horror on the Highway

Don Piper was killed instantly when a tractor trailer hit his Ford Escort head on crushing the small car. Paramedics covered Don's body with a tarp. Then Dick Onerecker, a minister, stopped and asked the paramedics if he could pray for Don.

"I walked over by the door, great physical damage on the outside and I laid my hands on him and began to pray for him."

As he knelt over the body, a sound came from beneath the tarp; after spending ninety minutes in heaven, Don had returned to life.

Please welcome back a very interesting guest, his name is Don Piper, it's good to see you Don, welcome.

Don Piper: Good to see you.

Interviewer: You were dead for ninety minutes, what happened.

Don Piper: I was on my way to church to lead a bible study, on a Wednesday and crossing a bridge in the middle of nowhere, an eighteen-wheeler crossed the centre stripe and literally ran over my car, just crushed it with me in it and I was killed instantly. It was just, you know, a hundred miles an hour of impact so there was no tunnel, I was just there. One moment, one second here, last breath, next second there, the gates of heaven.

Interviewer: That ain't a bad thing, ha ha!

Don Piper: No, it's a really good thing. I really didn't want to come back here.

Interviewer: Alright, what's it like, what did you see?

Don piper: It was the most real thing that's ever happened to me. I was standing at a gate. Of course scripture tells us there are twelve of these gates. I was at one, I was surrounded by people I had known and loved in life, who preceded me in death; and what a great reunion heaven is.

Interviewer: You saw family members?

Don Piper: Family members, teachers, classmates, I had gone to school with who had died at a young age. Uh, my next door neighbor was there. Uh, a lot of people I loved here and cared about here, but I probably would not have expected some of these people to greet me but they were there; and I think it's because they helped me get there. Yeah, God sent them out to greet me.

Interviewer: Well, that's the gate, you get inside; tell me what it's like.

Don Piper: Well actually I'm going through layers of aroma, layers of Angels, they're all over the place; ministering to the people of God bearing up the people of God. I went through music, unlike any I've ever heard here; probably thousands of songs at the same time and yet there was no chaos because they all fit together, they were all glorifying God.

Interviewer: What are Angels like?

Don Piper: Some had wings, some didn't. They were magnificently beautiful and they were bearing up people, they were surrounding me. I guess the most amazing thing about was the sound of their wings. You can actually hear the flutter and the holy whoosh of their wings.

Interviewer: The beggar Lazarus said he was carried by the Angels, were they carrying you?

Don Piper: Yes, absolutely. There was one in the car with me when I actually came back ninety minutes later I was holding the hand of an Angel; that's the only thing that really sustained me during that time so they were here; they are here and they were there to greet me and to bear me up so the Angels are magnificent servants of God. We don't become Angels of course when we go to heaven but I was carried by the angels to heaven.

Interviewer: Were they, I hate to use the term subservient, but the people of God; they are supposed to be on top...

Don Piper: They are; I got the distinct impression that they were taking care of me. They were ministering to me and they were the ones who delivered me to the very gates so when I was there, I knew the way I got there was by their bearing me up.

Interviewer: Did you see Jesus?

Don Piper: In the distance as I approached the gate, I'm looking through and there really is a golden street of course, uh quite incredible and structures that are more ornate than any I've ever seen here; inside the gates, uh but in the distance there is a kind of a hill, a pinnacle, high and lifted up in the middle of this city and at that point I could see the Lord, high and lifted up there at the top. A brilliant light that I couldn't have seen with earthly eyes, of course I didn't have earthly eyes, but you can see Him. What I really wanted to do is run down that street and up that hill and fall at His feet and say, "Thank-you for letting me be here!"

Interviewer: What did you do, what do people do when they get there?

Don Piper: Well you know there's...we'll dine at the Lord 's Table; we'll eat with Him but we won't gain weight, isn't that heavenly? So we'll dine, we'll sing together, we'll bless the Lord, we'll fellowship. I could imagine walking down that street of gold with Paul or Peter and just having a conversation with them. I really think that they'll be as glad to see us as we are to see them.

There's great fellowship in the Spirit. Not only is there praising God but there's the fellowship of the saints, they're gathered together. It's just the most exciting place I've ever seen. I can't imagine a place more exciting than heaven; very active.

Interviewer: No tears, no sorrow.

Don Piper: No, no pain, I wanna be in a place where there's no pain.

Interviewer: What about age?

Don Piper: There's no age. They were ageless, they were all fully developed humans, I wouldn't say adult because that's an Earth word. You know we have stages of life; there are no stages of life in heaven. We were fully developed, you know Adam and Eve were never children so I think that's the way God created us to have a relationship with him because that's what heaven is all about so they were age-less. The people I had I known here that were young in chronological age didn't look that young there and the people who were old here didn't look old either. They were ageless.

Interviewer: Well what about time?

Don Piper: There was no concept of time.

Interviewer: No time?

Don Piper: No, I was killed at 11:45 AM and I arrived back here at 1:15 PM and so that's ninety minutes in Earth time but in heaven, it is time-less. There's no concept of time. I could have been there for ninety years or ninety seconds, you just don't, it's linear propelled forward but there's no elapse of time because it's an eternal thing.

Interviewer: You didn't want to come back did you?

Don Piper: Oh not at all.

Interviewer: So why did you come back?

Don Piper: Well, people were praying that I would.

Interviewer: That's nice.

Don Piper: Yeah, they heard that I did and the gentleman that was behind me, behind the accident who was also a Pastor walked up to the bridge, we saw an interview with him Dick Onerecker; he had asked to pray for any of the victims and he was told they were all alright. They were four other victims. And they said well the man in the red car is dead; that was me. And God spoke to him and said, "Pray for the man in the red car". Well he never thought about praying for a dead man but he knew that God was speaking to him.

So he got permission to crawl in the car, put his hand on my right shoulder and he began to pray for me and sing hymns. Ninety minutes after that started signing "What a Friend We Have in Jesus" and I start singing it with him and he got out of the car really fast at that point and went over and said something to the effect, "The dead man is singing." Yeah, he had to convince them to do it.

So I came back to thirteen months in a hospital bed, thirty-four major surgeries, life and death on a day to day basis. I had to have external fixators placed on my arm and leg. It was a very, very long difficult...

Interviewer: Why didn't you get healed?

Don Piper: Well I'm healed to the extent that people can't believe I can still walk. Because I lost my leg, four inches of it and they had to attach; this arm was in the back seat of the car; so I'm healed that way. Uh, but you know what, I feel more healed and alive than I ever was before.

I don't recommend getting hit by a truck so you can have that experience but Jesus said we can have life abundantly here.

Interviewer: We had a question you know a couple of days ago. The Bible says it is appointed unto men once to die and after that judgment but what were you doing I mean?

Don Piper: I don't think I'm gonna die again. I think Jesus will come back before I die so I think I will have died once.

Interviewer: So that was the time?

Don Piper: I think that was it, yeah and I'm going back, I'm not coming back. It's good to be here with you but I'd rather be there. You know if you've been there, you wanna stay there. It's just the most real place of all.

Interviewer: Smells...

Don Piper: Yes, aromas that were sweet and luxurious, uh, I can still kind of remember what they smelled like and the sounds that I've heard there, and the people I embraced while I was there and the people; my grandfather extended his arms and said welcome home Donny.

Interviewer: You saw your grandfather?

Don Piper: I did, yeah I was with him when he died and he was there to greet me when I did; the cycle was complete.

Chapter 4 – On the Edge of Eternity

Herbert Broome died of cancer just hours after making this brief testimony. His family respected his wishes by sharing his last message with the world. On his deathbed he says that he was given a glimpse of heaven and hell; this is his story:

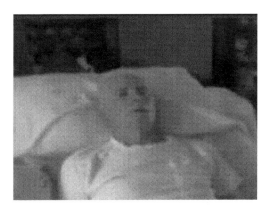

Interviewer: The other night, you were talking about when you were a security guard?

Herbert Broome: Yes.

Interviewer: And that it kind of gave you the idea for a ministry; about security?

Herbert Broome: Yes.

Interviewer: And well, just start with what your idea was.

Herbert Broome: My idea was that security is;... as a sinner you have absolutely no security...because everything changes, the world changes, the seasons change, everything changes. You clothes wear out, your job wears out; so can you think of anything that does not change? How are you going to get security in an unsecure world? Everything but one thing does not change.

Now if you are...how do you get security? The only way you can get that security and become a Christian is you have to accept Christ; you have to accept Him as He is. Must worship Him in spirit and truth, so you have to become a member of God's family, then you will have all the security you will ever need. Your security is where you are going to go when you die.

In this world we have the scriptures and why we have the Bible is because it's the only directions you need to become severely wise. So after then you can become into the family of God and now you have security.

The Bible says unless you are born again, you cannot see the kingdom of God. It says in the scriptures unless you're born again, you cannot enter into the heavens. Anyway, just being good and just saying you're a good fellow doesn't cut it because you cannot say you're living a good life and you're not hurting anybody; the point is you must be born again.

If you had seen what I saw in the hospital, there would be no doubt in your mind forever; because hell is so terrible, so awful. It goes as far as eternity; not just for a week or so but eternity forever and ever. Once you're in hell, you're in hell.

The Lord gave me a glimpse of heaven. I saw an Angel; I saw my Guardian Angel. And I also got a glimpse of hell and I'm telling you now, please listen; hell is so bad, so awful you have no idea how bad hell is; hell is terrible, a terrible place. I don't want to see anybody go there. I heard the murmurings, sounded like a thousand voices, all wailing at the same time, it was horrible.

Please listen, there was a white cloud, a mist came into the room; when I saw it was getting to me; as soon as it got to me everything was bliss, perfect bliss. I'm telling you now, you have to make a choice. I guess the thought would be to end my story, is you don't put your faith and trust in your money and your houses and material things. You have to put it in something that could never, never change and that's my story.

Afterword

Do you know someone who would be encouraged by reading this book? Perhaps you know someone that is mourning the loss of a loved one. Perhaps you have a friend or a family member that is facing their own mortality. If that is the case, I would ask you to give them a gift copy of this book. This book is published without any marketing or promotional budget so it is only by word-of-mouth sharing and giving that will allow it to reach others. By sending a gift copy, you can inspire and encourage them and even give them hope for eternity.

What do people care about today? What question must every person ask at some time in their lives? – Is heaven for real? They may not ask this question when they are young and carefree. They may not ask it today or tomorrow but you can rest assured that some day they will ask that question and they will want to find an answer. You have the answer that they are looking for.

When someone you know asks that question, "Is Heaven for Real?" will you be able to pass along this information?

I would like to tell you the story of a young college student who was ambitiously pursuing his own plans for life. He thought he was following a path towards success but the distractions of the world were bringing life-threatening dangers towards him from many different directions.

One day someone gave that young man a book; it was a simple little book about the end-time events as described in Revelation from the Bible. That book planted a seed that took root and over the course of several months, that young man slowly came to faith and escaped from the negative influences that were threatening to destroy his life. That young man was me! You never know how a simple little book can turn out to be a treasure for someone.

Now you also have a simple treasure that you can easily share with others. Freely you have received, freely give (Matthew 10 v 8). All you need is someone's email address and you can send a gift copy of this book to them that they can read on their Kindle Reader, on their portable device or even on their desktop computer. It is also available in paperback so you can send them a hard copy to read. Of course you can share the powerful message of hope in many ways other than this book; especially non-verbally with actions of love and kindness.

One may wonder, is it worthwhile to think about heaven? Is it useful to share stories about heaven? Some would argue against it. Some have even made the comment, "He is so heavenly minded, he is no earthly good!" This is simply a negative comment that is unproductive. The Apostle Paul wrote in Philippians:

*I press toward the mark for the prize of the high calling of God in Christ Jesus. Let us therefore, as many as be perfect, be thus minded...**let us mind the same*** *thing...For many walk, of whom I have told you often, and now tell you even weeping, that they are the enemies of the cross of Christ: Whose end is destruction, whose God is their belly, and whose glory is in their shame, who mind earthly things.*

Paul tells us to mind the same thing, the prize, what the Amplified Bible calls the supreme and **heavenly** prize. He actually has harsh words for those who mind earthly things. We look to hope, a hope that makes not ashamed, the hope that is laid up for you in Heaven and you can be sure... "...every man that hath this hope in Him purifies himself, even as he is pure".

To be heavenly minded on the contrary can bring much earthly good! – Being heavenly minded fosters an awareness of how important it is to love one another, to encourage one another towards good deeds as we know the day is fast approaching.

So, this book is simply a tool to encourage and open up discussion but it can be much more. Imagine the effect you could have for all of eternity; you have the opportunity to strengthen the faith of a believer who is struggling; you can lead an unbeliever to the glorious hope of heaven and at the same time you will build up rewards in heaven for yourself and strengthen your own steadfast hope.

If you sent a gift copy of this book to just a few friends; what an impact that could make on someone's life for eternity? What blessed hope could take root and grow! There are people you can reach that no one else can. Please share this treasure with others; here are the links for you:

Is Heaven for Real? Personal Stories of Visiting Heaven

http://www.amazon.com/dp/B00BXKG41U

and the second volume:

Is Heaven for Real? 2: Personal Stories of Visiting Heaven

http://www.amazon.com/dp/B00CTT66SU

May God richly bless you in all things.

~ Patrick Doucette

42151823R00112

Made in the USA
San Bernardino, CA
27 November 2016